PAST LIVES FUTURE LIVES

Accounts of regression
and progression
through hypnosis.

Dr. Bruce Goldberg

NEWCASTLE PUBLISHING CO., INC.
North Hollywood, California
1982

ACKNOWLEDGMENTS

I would like to thank Harry Martin, Edie House, and all of the people who work at WBAL-TV, Sallee Rigler and WRC Radio, Charlie Donovan and WFBR Radio, my editors Victoria Pasternack and Douglas Menville, and others too numerous to mention, for their cooperation and thoughtfulness.

FIRST EDITION
A NEWCASTLE ORIGINAL
First Printing June 1982
3 4 5 6 7 8 9 10

Printed in the United States of America

CONTENTS

DEDICATION

This book is dedicated to all my patients (past, present, and future), without whom it would not have been possible.

INTRODUCTION

The purpose of *Past Lives—Future Lives* is to present the idea of reincarnation and karma to the reader in an attempt to explain why we are here and how we can all better ourselves. It is not my purpose to try to convert anyone to a belief in parapsychology or to interfere in any way with your particular religious or spiritual preferences.

If, however, you are not satisfied with traditional concepts of birth and death, then this book might very well change your life. Those of you who have ever wondered what it is like to die and what choices—if any—you will be given after death will begin to find answers to your questions.

In this book I use actual case histories of past-life regression, along with progressions into future lives to help explain the laws of karma. Everyone has a karmic cycle, and the better we understand it, the easier our lives will be. This is my real purpose in writing this book—to help people understand why they do what they do and show them how to avoid making the same mistakes over and over again. If this book can help even one reader better his or her karmic cycle, then the time and energy spent in my research and writing will have been justified.

Whenever I use hypnosis to regress a patient into a past life or progress him or her into the future, I achieve a greater understanding of human behavior and the human mind than I could possibly obtain from any other source. In addition, the mechanisms of the karmic cycle begin to make so much more sense, and I am better able to offer my patients guidance.

It is not the purpose of this book to either prove or disprove the concept of reincarnation. Even with all the cases that have been recorded, there are still people who will doubt its validity. That is every person's right. It is my purpose, however, to enlighten the public to the effectiveness of hypnotic regression and progression. Even after the American Medical Association's formal acceptance of hypnosis in 1958, there have been relatively few practitioners of the technique. Misinformation about hypnosis must be replaced with accurate knowledge of this tremendously therapeutic discipline. The laws of supply and demand will then increase the number of hypnotherapists.

My own experience using hypnosis therapeutically has established and confirmed my belief in reincarnation. I have not been overly influenced by Eastern religion, gurus, or occultists. I have been influenced by the success I have had in helping people help themselves. Reincarnation and the laws of karma most logically explain the results I have witnessed using hypnotherapy.

If a patient's fear of heights, for example, can be traced back to falling off a cliff in a past life, and if reliving this scene permanently removes this fear, then who am I to question the validity of the scene? The most important point here is the elimination of the problem.

When trying to explain our purpose on this planet, traditional theories fall short, in my opinion. Karma is a logical explanation to me and I hope it will be informative to you.

Note: Some of the minor details in the case histories have been altered to protect the privacy of my patients. All the names used, except the chapters on the regressions and progressions of Harry Martin, have been altered. Everything else in these pages is true.

CHAPTER ONE

THE PAST LIVES OF A TV TALK SHOW HOST

On a cold and overcast Wednesday afternoon in March of 1980, Harry Martin began his journey into the past.

From the moment he arrived at my office, Harry made it clear that he was very skeptical about hypnosis and even more skeptical about past-life regressions. Yet I could tell that this 28-year-old TV talk show co-host was a highly intelligent man with great powers of concentration—which made him, potentially at least, an excellent candidate for hypnosis. (Being skeptical about regressions has very little to do with one's ability to be regressed. The suggestibility of the patient and the doctor-patient rapport determines success or failure in regression therapy.)

After explaining what hypnosis is—or rather, what it *isn't*—I induced a hypnotic trance, told Harry he would remember everything upon awakening, and used simple age regression to bring Harry back to the age of five. He described a scene in which he drew a circle on a cardboard box and pretended that it was a television set. He was trying to impress a six-year-old female playmate, an "older woman," of his communication abilities. Even at this young age Harry showed interest in television as a career. The details of this scene, as Harry remembered it, were very vivid. He described the clothes he was wearing, the color of the crayon that he used to draw the TV set, and the weather that day.

This was a very good session, and after it was over much of Harry's skepticism about hypnosis—though not about past-life regression—had vanished. (Later Harry would tell me on my second "Hello Baltimore" appearance that if it hadn't been for my credentials as a dentist and my overall reputation he would never have participated in this project.)

The second session was held two weeks later. It was a lovely spring afternoon, and a second simple age regression was performed. This time Harry was taken back to age two. He saw and described some very detailed scenes at his grandmother's house. After the regression was over he expressed concern over some of the information he reported. For one thing, the color of the wallpaper in the bedroom he saw conflicted with what he consciously remembered. Second, the doorbell was different from what he could recall now.

I suggested he check out this information for its accuracy with his grandmother. I also gave him a "conditioning" tape for past-life regression which consisted of a verbal induction into hypnosis and suggestions for the subconscious mind to explore its memory banks for any information that it would like to discover. The subconscious mind has a perfect memory bank. Since this vast storehouse is tappable only when the conscious mind (see Chapter 2) is relaxed and set aside, use of a "conditioning tape" allows a patient to access this information more easily. I told Harry to play the tape in a completely waking state first, to make sure it wouldn't lead him into a life that was pure imagination. A completely waking state consists of the conscious mind functioning along with the subconscious mind. In the hypnotic state the subconscious mind works by itself (see Chapter 2). The tape contains no leading suggestions and by listening to it out of trance, the patient will feel more confident about the subsequent impressions he receives.

Before the next session, Harry called excitedly to inform me of several positive events. First, he had played my tape in a waking state and was satisfied with its purpose. Second, while playing the tape one night he experienced another age regression. Third, he had verified the details of the scene at his grandmother's house. The doorbell and the wallpaper were in fact as he saw them in the regression, not as he consciously remembered. (This demonstrates how uncannily accurate our subconscious mind's memory bank is.)

In the first week in April, Harry came to my office for what was to be his first past-life regression. After some discussion about his progress with my "conditioning" tape, we went into my hypnotherapy room for the regression. Harry seemed quite calm, but indicated some surprise that I wasn't the least bit nervous. My hypnotherapy room is equipped with a recliner for the patient and a desk and chair for myself. I have a revolving disc that I have the patient look at to help induce a hypnotic trance. The temperature of the room is slightly warmer than normal, which also facilitates trance induction.

The trance was induced and I asked Harry what he saw. (Unfortunately these preliminary sessions weren't tape-recorded, but I recall details of the regressions.) He described a ship but couldn't make out any details at first. The scene he was describing was simply a ship approaching a dock on an island. Once the problem of orienting himself to this scene was overcome, much information concerning this scene and the surrounding circumstances was obtained.

This ship, called *The Dove*, was a cargo ship in the 18th century. Harry's name was Michael Bartholomew. In 1740, Michael was brought to this island to take over the shipping operation. The warehouse that stored the cargo was owned by Michael's uncle, but upon the uncle's death, Michael had inherited it.

Harry reported many scenes depicting Michael hard at work running the warehouse. Much of the physical work of loading and unloading cargo, as well as all of the supervisory functions, were carried out by Michael. (It is interesting to note that in his present life, Harry is an extremely hard worker and very much involved with the production end of television, along with being co-host of his talk show. His karmic pattern has remained consistent.)

After he came out of the trance, Harry made another observation. Just as I was about to ask him a question ("What is happening now?"), he told me the answer ("I'm going to the other side of the island to check on some workmen"). I considered it an illustration of telepathy. This is a common experience and does not require a very deep trance to be noted. All in all he was very pleased with this regression and so was I. It seemed to be evidence of a former life Harry had lived nearly 250 years before. Still, I don't know exactly how much of his skepticism concerning past-life regression was removed. But I was convinced that progress was being made.

Harry was very enthusiastic that day as he left my office with an appointment to see me the following Monday for another past-life regression.

When he came to my office for the next session, he looked a little tired but was still looking forward to the regression.

The second past-life regression actually went better than the first. Harry was in a somewhat deeper trance and now he was used to the experience. But the first thing he saw—or didn't see —very much surprised him. Remember, these sessions were not taped, so only fragments of the actual dialogue will be given.

Dr. Goldberg: What do you see?
Harry: I, I don't see anything.
Dr. Goldberg: Take a moment and let any scene materialize slowly.
Harry: Oh my God. The reason I can't see anything is because I am blind.

This illustrates an important principle of regression therapy. Even though Harry was blind in this particular life, he was made aware of that fact immediately and could still see the environment he was in. In other words, if you lack the use of your sight or hearing in a past life, you can still perceive your environment by the use of the hypnotic trance state.

It seems that Harry's name was Hap in this life, and he was born blind in 1847 on a farm in Utah. At the age of four he was brought to a small Western town where he learned to play the piano. Eventually he earned his living by playing piano in the bar of the hotel in which he lived. Even though he was blind, a situation that many people would find highly undesirable, he enjoyed his life. Harry described a scene in which Hap had gone for a walk in the woods just outside of the town and had gotten lost. It took him about three hours to use his other highly developed senses to find his way back to town.

What is interesting to note about this past life is Hap's creativity. In his present life, Harry is very creative and, although he doesn't play the piano, he does play the drums. Harry is also writing a novel. Thus, his karmic pattern of creativity, as well as hard work, is consistently exhibited.

Near the end of Hap's life, he developed arthritis in both of his hands and was unable to play the piano. He described scenes in which he would go down to the bar and listen to the new piano player. Instead of feeling bitter or showing remorse, Hap's attitude was extremely positive and pleasant. This also coincides with Harry's present constructive attitude and pleasantness (obviously important qualities for a talk show host—the ability to make his guests feel welcome, relaxed, and to express interest and appreciation at all times).

Harry seemed very pleased with the results of this regression and said he could definitely relate to the emotions he felt as Hap.

It was two weeks later when I saw Harry again for another past-life regression. This was to be his third and last regression, and you will shortly see that it was a most significant session.

The date was April 28, and it was a Monday. Earlier that day I had received a telephone call from one of my patients informing me that much of the information we obtained from her last age regression had checked out with members of her family. This is always most satisfying to hear, of course.

Harry arrived on time and after reviewing some of the karmic principles he illustrated in the previous two past-life regressions, I induced him into a very deep trance.

Harry described a life as an English radio operator for the Royal Air Force during World War II. He was born in 1907. The plane he was flying was a bomber. He spent a great deal of time describing the plane. (Harry has no present interest in planes.) As the scenes progressed, it became obvious that this plane was to play an important part in this particular life.

Most of his World War II experience for the R.A.F. centered on North Africa. The last year he mentioned to me was 1945, so I progressed him five years forward. This is what he reported:

Dr. Goldberg:	Where do you find yourself now?
Harry:	I am lying on this table of some sort and as I look up all I can see is a large dome. It is hard to make it out clearly because of the brightness of the light.
Dr. Goldberg:	What color is the light?
Harry:	White.
Dr. Goldberg:	Are you alone?
Harry:	No. I can't see anyone, but I can hear people talking about me.
Dr. Goldberg:	What are they saying?

Harry:	They are evaluating my life, my life as the radio operator. I must have died.

I then asked him to go back to the last day of his life as the radio operator.

Dr. Goldberg:	What do you see?
Harry:	I'm on a raft. The plane, it went down—crashed.
Dr. Goldberg:	Is anyone with you on the raft?
Harry:	No, I'm alone.
Dr. Goldberg:	What year is it?
Harry:	1949.

Harry reported having been on this raft for a number of days. His food and water supplies had run out and he was dying. He described his position on the raft as being "sprawled out," with his arms and legs hanging over the sides. He saw himself slowly die, but was not upset by it. (This is a common response because the patient realizes there is nothing he can do about the situation.) Harry then described a very dry feeling in his mouth and throat in the present time. I brought him to the point just after he had died and further questioned him.

Dr. Goldberg:	What do you feel now?
Harry:	I feel very strange. I feel as if I'm floating and it's as if I no longer have a body.
Dr. Goldberg:	How do your throat and mouth feel?
Harry:	I no longer feel thirsty. It's just very peaceful here.

This is again a common description. All physical discomforts are removed once the patient has died in the past life.

What is interesting to note about this regression is Harry's description of the in-between-life state. The dome that Harry described to me is similar to what has been told to me before by other patients. I have never seen it described in any other book or account of past-life regression. Furthermore, Harry is admittedly very skeptical about reincarnation and has read no books about it. (He hadn't even heard of the Bridey Murphy story.) So this confirmed the authenticity of the regression for me.

Another interesting note about this regression is that Harry reported dying in 1949. In this life he was born on June 14, 1951. He had two years in between lives. This is a rather short time.

I asked him finally in trance what he felt he had achieved in his last life. He said he hadn't achieved enough; he felt bad about not leaving his mark on the world. As the RAF radio operator, he had never married and had no family to speak of. Today, Harry is married and is well on his way to leaving his mark on the world. His present life appears to be the culmination of a number of his past lives.

After the session was over, Harry and I discussed this particular regression in detail. He described the strange feeling he experienced in the dome as well as right after he had died. Still the plane stood out as the most significant aspect of that life.

This ended the past-life regressions, but I wanted Harry to come back one more time to show him how deep into his subconscious he could go without regressing into a former life. He was scheduled to return in ten days.

During that week I went to the library and found books with photographs of World War II airplanes from various countries. At his next visit, I showed these books to Harry. He immediately identified the plane he had seen during the hypnotic regression. It was indeed an English World War II bomber.

In this final session, Harry was induced into a very deep hypnotic trance. I gave him a series of relaxation suggestions but this time I did not say that he was to remember everything upon awakening, as I had said in all of the previous sessions, though I didn't say that he was to forget anything either.

When he came out of the trance, he said he felt absolutely great. Also, he could not remember anything of what I said to him while he was in the trance. He felt as if he had been under for more than an hour. In actuality it was only about twenty minutes. This time distortion is quite common during trances, especially deeper trance levels.

We then discussed my appearing on his television show to educate the public about the clinical benefits of hypnosis. We agreed to meet and work out the details, and Harry left my office. On his way home an interesting thing happened. While stopped at a red light, Harry looked up and saw a World War II airplane very similar to the one he had seen in his last past-life regression.

He had never seen that plane before, either in Baltimore or anywhere else to the best of his knowledge. It seems this plane was out to haunt him, because a few days later he again saw this type of plane on a news assignment in Delaware. When Harry called me to report these events, my conclusion was simply that that particular past life was important to his karmic growth, and the reappearance of the plane was a reminder of his lessons learned and those he has still to learn.

There is an ancient saying, "When the student is ready, the teacher will be there." Until he met me, Harry had been very skeptical about parapsychology and past-life regressions. He was not ready. After experiencing regressions personally, Harry quickly learned how accurate and significant they can be. The student was ready and the teacher was there.

My experience with Harry came about as a result of my desire to clear up the public's misconceptions about hypnosis. Unfortunately, Hollywood films over the years have portrayed hypnosis in a very negative and inaccurate fashion. Newspapers and magazines have done a more credible job, but because of its massive appeal and influence over the American public, I wanted to use the exposure of television to discuss hypnosis and its use in past-life regression.

The major obstacle I faced was how to interest a television station in doing a show on hypnosis and regression in an ethical and true-to-life depiction of the experience. I decided to call the local NBC* affiliate in Baltimore to discuss the idea. I spoke with the assignment editor in the news department and told her I was a local dentist who had a separate practice in hypnotherapy. In addition, I mentioned my involvement with past-life regression therapy and my training from the American Society of Clinical Hypnosis. She seemed intrigued by my story. She asked me to come down to the studio to discuss it with her.

On a very cold Friday afternoon in early December of 1979, I arrived at WBAL and spoke with the assignment editor, Beverly Marable. She was very cordial, but concerned about whether I could actually do what I said I could do with hypnosis. I understood her attitude and suggested I regress an employee of the studio to establish my credibility with them firsthand. She agreed to this and volunteered herself as the patient. I was delighted. If

---

*On August 31, 1981, WBAL-TV changed its affiliation from NBC to CBS.

I regressed her, there could be no question of fraud or collusion.

During our first appointment, Beverly was regressed to the age of five and described, in very great detail, a trip to San Francisco she had made by train. After the trance was over, she was amazed at how she was able to recall all the details, details which she would not have been able to recall consciously. A second appointment was made. She left my office feeling refreshed and somewhat astonished at what she had just experienced.

Ms. Marable came to my office for her next session. All her skepticism had vanished. She was quite a good hypnotic patient, though the information that was obtained during her past-life regression was somewhat sketchy. Nonetheless, she was impressed with the results.

The scene she described consisted of an early 1800s one-room schoolhouse. Since she was a devout city dweller, with no personal experience in rural settings, she knew that she could not have, or would not be likely to, imagine such a scene. She left my office feeling a bit mystified, but told me the producer of "Hello Baltimore" would call me and set up an appointment for one of their on-the-air personalities to experience a number of regressions so that he could describe his subjective experiences on the air. I couldn't ask for a more ideal situation. It would completely remove any thoughts of hoax, and provide me with an interviewer who could publicly verify the validity of his experience with me during hypnosis.

Harry Martin's case history, which began this chapter, established my credibility with the producers as a practitioner of past-lives hypnotherapy.

We were now prepared to do the show on Monday, May 19, 1980. I wasn't nervous (one of the many advantages of self-hypnosis), but I was very much excited about this appearance.

I arrived at the studio at 11:00 A.M., in time to get acquainted with the other co-host, Edie House, a very attractive young woman with a relaxed manner about her, immaculately dressed and very soft-spoken. We didn't have much time to talk before the show, but I knew that Harry had briefed her about my work and his experiences.

The show went rather well. The hosts and I discussed hypnosis and past-life regression, and then I answered questions from viewers who called in.

The response to the show was unbelievable. Hundreds of telephone calls came into the studio and, to my surprise, all the calls were positive. The only complaints the studio received were that I was not on long enough. Viewers requested that the videotape of my interview be repeated.

Two days later, I received a telephone call from a talk show host of a Washington, D.C., radio show, wanting me to discuss hypnosis and past-life regression a couple of weeks hence. I felt like a local celebrity.

My second appearance on "Hello Baltimore" was on July 28. When I arrived at the studio on this very hot and humid summer day, I could sense a difference in Harry and Edie. We all felt more relaxed and spontaneous.

During the show I established some of the basic concepts of reincarnation and illustrated how they could be used in hypnotherapy to remove the causes of certain habits, and especially phobias. Harry's skepticism about reincarnation again surfaced.

Harry: Even though I went through this, there is still a bit of skepticism about this. How do I know that what I really experienced isn't something that I experienced before, something that I read in a book or saw in a movie or on TV?

Dr. Goldberg: There are two differences between a regression and a fantasy, or just use of your own imagination as in a daydream. One difference, and you can relate to the lives we took you through, is that in a regression you feel the scene. You don't just say that I'm in a Western scene or in an airplane, you actually feel the emotions involved. If you're happy, you feel happy and if you're sad you feel sad. In a daydream if you see yourself on the beach, for example, you will imagine that scene but you won't sweat or feel thirsty. In a regression you feel the scene. The second thing is the ability to almost read minds. Harry, you illustrated this telepathy yourself. You were able to know even before I asked you a question what I was going to ask you. Do you remember that?

| Harry: | That's right. That did happen. |
| Dr. Goldberg: | This form of telepathy cannot be imagined. |

We don't know the exact mechanism of telepathy. It is sometimes exhibited in hypnotic trances, especially past-life regression
trances. However, we do know that the trance state facilitates
various forms of psychic phenomena. Telepathy is one of these.

I do not profess to have made an absolute believer out of Harry,
nor was it my purpose. My purpose was simply to show the
difference between a fantasy and a regression. (The use of regression has gained so much respect of late that it is sometimes used
in court as evidence and by many police departments to obtain
evidence.)

Later that summer, Sallee Rigler, a psychic from Aberdeen,
Maryland, appeared on "Hello Baltimore." I had occasion to
watch the show and I was impressed with her. Sallee hosts a
weekend radio show in Washington, D.C. Just two days later I
received a call from Sallee's producer at WRC Radio. They wanted
me to appear on Sallee's show to discuss past-life regression. I
could sense that all this exposure represented a new beginning
for me and my work.

CHAPTER TWO

WHAT IS HYPNOSIS?

Hypnosis is a subject of great interest to nearly everyone. The fascination it holds is its promise to open a world of hidden treasure and self-improvement, as if by magic. And nearly everyone finds at some time he has a desire or need to improve himself. Hypnosis sounds like an easy answer. After all, the hypnotist has the power to make people do things (like learning a foreign language) or stop doing things (like smoking or overeating). Doesn't he?

Actually, the hypnotist has no power and never did. He or she just has a special skill. Yet the misconception is understandable. Skilled hypnotists in the past were professional entertainers. They deliberately tried to give the false impression that they had a "remarkable power" over the subject and could force him to do bizarre things. The only real power behind hypnosis lies with the subject and his mind.

MY OWN STORY

Many people ask me how a dentist got involved in such controversial fields as hypnosis and parapsychology. (Especially past-life regression and progression into future lives.) It didn't happen by coincidence, but by synchronicity.

As a child I always knew that dentistry was to be my career. By the age of six I had made this decision.

During my childhood and adolescence I showed no interest in parapsychology or hypnosis. By college age I chose a school that had an excellent biology department. As a biology major with a chemistry minor I was being well trained for dental school, but certainly not for work as a hypnotherapist.

During my four years at college I was exposed to many philosophies and belief systems; however, my attitude toward parapsychology was always objective. I didn't accept or reject it. Like a good scientist, I merely considered the data neutrally. Hypnosis and karma were simply not part of my interests.

My freshman year in dental school consisted of dentistry and little else. During my second year I investigated astrology by taking a course in it, and read my first accounts of past-life regression using hypnosis. My interest stirred. During the remainder of my dental school career I spent more time researching parapsychology. I fed a lot of information into my subconscious memory banks.

What is of karmic significance is that I had natural talents in these disciplines. After graduation I entered a general practice dental residency at a Florida state hospital. (Residencies are not required in dentistry but they are nice to have as part of one's background.) It was here that an opportunity presented itself that was to change my life. A brochure from the American Society of Clinical Hypnosis offered a course in hypnosis to be given in Jackson, Mississippi. I had plenty of vacation time stored up, so I decided to attend. These courses are offered only to dentists, physicians, and psychologists. I was in good company. One of the psychiatrists who trained me told me I had a natural gift for hypnosis. He encouraged me to use it in my practice. My intention was to use it on my dental patients to reduce their apprehension and, in certain cases, to replace chemical anesthesia.

What he didn't know was that I had read up on past-life regression, and one of the first things I intended to do after the course was completed was to use hypnosis to prove or disprove reincarnation—to my own satisfaction. It was no coincidence that I received the brochure from the American Society of Clinical Hypnosis at that time, and it was certainly no coincidence that the very first patient I hypnotized when I got back to Tallahassee regressed into a former lifetime.

The patient was a young lady I knew well. She expressed great interest in hypnosis and asked me to regress her. I agreed. She was a somnambule, a very deep hypnotic patient, and she described a number of past lives to me. She even spoke several foreign languages fluently while in the trance state. I knew enough of her background to know that she knew nothing about past lives, hypnosis, or foreign languages. These regressions occurred over a period of about three months. Each session lasted between forty-five minutes and an hour.

That did it. I was already excited by hypnosis, but more than that, I became a believer in reincarnation and karma from that day on.

From a mathematical point of view, the odds must be millions to one against my hypnosis training and my first hypnotic patient being so successful, all within a period of about three weeks. Immediately I began using hypnosis with my dental patients at the hospital for elimination of apprehension toward their dental treatment. In some cases I used hypnosis in place of chemical anesthesia (novocaine). The hospital approved of my hypnotic techniques and their application to dentistry.

I also used hypnosis for habit elimination, relief of minor medical problems, and then phobias on patients not connected with the hospital but referred to me by former patients. During this time I also successfully regressed various people into past lives. I was quickly obtaining a reputation concerning my clinical uses of hypnosis.

In June of 1976 I moved to Baltimore to set up my dental and hypnosis practices. In March of 1980, Harry Martin of WBAL-TV was in my office waiting to be taken back into a past life. It was part of my karmic cycle to succeed with him and to bring karma and past-life regression via television and radio to the attention of the Baltimore-Washington metropolitan area.

HYPNOSIS AND THE INNER WORKINGS OF THE MIND

A simple definition of hypnosis is "a state of increased suggestibility accompanied by a focusing of one's concentration on one thought, idea, or person." When I say "increased suggestibility," I must explain that a person in a hypnotic trance will only accept suggestions that he or she might normally accept when not in a trance state. We all possess a moral and ethical code which cannot be violated regardless of the depth of the hypnotic trance.

To understand what hypnosis is, one must consider the inner workings of the human mind. Our mind is made up of four different levels of activity.

The first level or stage is called *Beta*. This is the level of complete consciousness. We function in this level approximately sixteen hours each day. The main purpose of this level is to regulate our life-controlling bodily functions, such as heartbeat, breathing, kidney functions, digestion, etc. About 75 percent of the Beta level or conscious mind proper is spent monitoring these vital bodily functions. Thus, only 25 percent of the conscious mind is left to deal with what we know as our conscious thoughts.

The second level is what we call *Alpha*. Alpha corresponds to the subconscious mind, and this is what we deal with in hypnosis. This level is characterized by 95–100 percent concentration efficiency. This is far superior to the 25 percent efficiency of the conscious, or Beta, level. Examples of activity on the Alpha level are hypnosis, meditation, biofeedback, daydreaming, crossing over into natural sleep, and awakening. Hypnosis is a natural state of mind. It is not sleep. You are fully aware when you are hypnotized.

The next level of mental activity is called *Theta*. This is the part of the unconscious mind that functions in light sleep. The term *conscious* means awake and aware; *unconscious* means unawake and unaware.

The last level is called *Delta*. This corresponds to deep sleep. At this level, the unconscious mind is obtaining the greatest amount of rest. Suggestions will not be heard at this level. This level lasts approximately 30 to 40 minutes each night.

CONSCIOUS MIND PROPER (BETA)	LIGHT SLEEP (THETA)
SUBCONSCIOUS (ALPHA)	DEEP SLEEP (DELTA)
CONSCIOUS MIND	UNCONSCIOUS MIND

FIGURE 1

In summary, the mind consists of four levels. When we get up in the morning we have just gone from natural hypnosis (Alpha) to full consciousness (Beta). When we go to sleep at night we go from Beta (full consciousness) to Alpha (natural hypnosis) to Theta (light sleep) to Delta (deep sleep) to Theta (light sleep) to Alpha, and the cycle repeats itself.

THE EXPERIENCE OF BEING HYPNOTIZED

If you are hypnotized, you will be in the Alpha state. What will you experience? Exactly what is the hypnotic trance like?

Hypnosis is simply setting aside conscious mind, and dealing with the subconscious mind directly. At no time will you be asleep.

When we are functioning at full consciousness (Beta), both the subconscious and conscious minds are functioning (see Figure 1). The physical experience in hypnosis will be identical to that of full consciousness, with three exceptions.

First, your concentration will be more focused, nearly 100 percent as compared to the 25 percent efficiency of the conscious mind. Second, every muscle in your body will feel relaxed. (Some people feel a floating sensation, others a warm or tingling feeling. Most people feel a heaviness, especially in the arms and legs.) Third, there is what I call "immobility." This is not technically accurate because one is always able to move any part of the body at any time. The patient in hypnosis doesn't *want* to move, so he or she doesn't. Many people have compared this effect to having laughing gas (nitrous oxide) in the dentist's office. This is quite accurate because nitrous oxide will place a patient in a hypnotic trance chemically.

Thus, a hypnotized patient will experience increased concentration, complete relaxation, and lack of movement. Also, our senses are more developed in trance, so that the sense of hearing, touch, smell, etc. will be more accurate in a hypnotic trance state. That's it. There will be no levitation, skyrockets or any kind of sleep or zombie effect. Examples of natural, day-to-day hypnosis include daydreaming, crossing over into natural sleep at night, the beginning stages of waking up from natural sleep in the morning, watching most television, watching windshield wipers on a rainy night, watching light posts or white lines on a highway at night (highway hypnosis), reading a novel and getting so involved in the plot that you lose track of time.

Think about a daydream for a moment. When you daydream you are focusing your mind on a person, place or event which is usually pleasant. You are not concerned about the weather, what time it is, or whether your clothes are too loose or too tight. If someone were in the same room with you while you were daydreaming, they would probably have to snap their fingers and call your name to get your attention. This is the Alpha state and the best example of natural hypnosis. Everyone daydreams, and most people spend between one and two hours daydreaming every day. Thus, most people spend at least two hours every day in natural hypnosis. Hypnosis is thus a natural and normal state of mind. There is absolutely no danger involved.

In fact, since our senses are more developed or sharper, we are less prone to accidents or other forms of injury when we are in hypnosis. I am not aware of any instances in which hypnosis has ever resulted in either psychological or physical harm to a patient. A person who has a car accident late at night might be the victim of highway hypnosis, but only because he would normally have been asleep while he was behind the wheel.

In this book I will be showing you how hypnosis can be used to relive very traumatic incidents in a person's present, past or future life with no negative side effects. In fact, many positive effects result, such as the elimination of fears, habits, and other negative tendencies.

THE LEVELS OF HYPNOSIS

Now, what about the different levels or stages of hypnosis? Today scientists classify over twenty different levels of hypnosis, but for simplicity I will divide hypnosis into three main levels.

The first is called *light trance*. In this level the patient is relaxed and probably won't feel that he or she is hypnotized. Although regressions and progressions can be accomplished at this level, the information obtained is very sketchy. In addition, when I work with phobias (fears), habits, depression, etc., this level has only limited efficiency in accepting very complex or difficult suggestions. Ninety-five to ninety-eight percent of the public can achieve this level.

The second level is called *medium trance*. This is the level in which I prefer to work. In this level the patient is more completely relaxed and more able to accept very difficult or complex suggestions. He can more easily relive and actually feel an event or scene in regression or progression. At this level the patient may be aware of outside noises but it will not distract him. About 70 percent of the public can achieve this level.

The last level is called deep or *somnambulistic trance*. This is the level of hypnosis a stage hypnotist likes to use because one characteristic of it is "hypnoamnesia." In other words, the patient will not remember what he or she did or said in trance unless specifically told to remember upon awakening. Only about 5 or 10 percent of the public can achieve this level. This level is also characterized by positive hallucinations (seeing an object that is not really there) as well as negative hallucinations (not being able to see an object that is there).

Even in this very deep level, however, the patient cannot be told to do or say anything that is against his or her moral or ethical code. So you see, a hypnotized person is never under anyone's control but his own. Unless I am interested in documenting a regression or involved in other types of research, I do not prefer to work with a patient at this level. It is not dangerous, merely unnecessary.

WHO CAN BE HYPNOTIZED?

As I have already mentioned, 95 percent of the public can be placed in at least a light hypnotic trance. People often ask me to describe the kind of people who make the best hypnotic patients and those that cannot be hypnotized. The best hypnotic patients are intelligent people (contrary to the popular misconception) who have an excellent memory, can focus their concentration, visualize scenes with great detail, can express emotions easily, are not overly critical, and who can go to a lecture or movie and become so deeply involved in the plot that time passes very quickly. Children make excellent patients because of their imagination, respect for authority and lack of resistance or skepticism.

The best hypnotic patients are children between the ages of eight and sixteen.

Those people who usually make the worst hypnotic patients are people who have very short attention spans, tend to focus on the past and future rather than the present, are overly critical, use logic instead of emotions, have lower I.Q.'s, and have great difficulty "letting themselves go." Mental retardation, senility, brain damage, inability to understand the language of the hypnotist, and overly cynical attitudes are also going to prevent the induction of a hypnotic trance.

SELF-HYPNOSIS

When I discuss hypnosis, I refer to *self-hypnosis*. All hypnosis is actually self-hypnosis. It is impossible to hypnotize someone against their will, unless certain drugs are used. I never recommend or use drugs. Thus, during a hypnotic session, a patient learns how to hypnotize himself, utilizing the services of a hypnotherapist. The term for this is *heterohypnosis*, meaning hypnosis by another (*hetero* means "other"). Even the most skillful hypnotherapist is unable to hypnotize someone against his or her will.

All of my patients are taught self-hypnosis so that they can condition themselves for deeper trance levels and shorten the time it takes to induce the hypnotic trance. I record cassette tapes for all of my patients so that they can be exposed daily to the suggestions that I give them at their weekly sessions. There are many ways to learn self-hypnosis, but I find the use of cassette tapes to be the most efficient.

OUR OWN NATURAL COMPUTER

Hypnosis takes place in the Alpha state, or subconscious mind, which is best described as a computer. Just as a computer is programmed or fed information, the subconscious mind is constantly undergoing a programming process. Everything that our five senses can detect, as well as extrasensory perception (E.S.P.), is permanently stored in the subconscious mind's memory bank. Since the subconscious mind, along with the conscious mind,

functions for about sixteen hours each day, scientists estimate
that the average human brain is exposed to, and stores, 1,000,000
separate pieces of information every day.

Each piece of information is stored in what is termed a "memory trace" in the brain. If you multiply 1,000,000 by 365, and
then multiply this total by your age, then you have an idea of
how many memory traces you are using. Scientists estimate that
the average human mind contains 70 trillion memory traces.
Since a trillion is a thousand billion, and a billion is a thousand
million, you can see that even a 70-year-old person has barely
used his potential of memory traces.

When I use hypnosis to regress patients into past lives, I attempt
to tap into the memory traces of their subconscious minds and
bring to their conscious awareness the stored sensory data that
will reveal the origin of their present habits, phobias, or negative
tendencies. By reliving these past experiences they permanently
eliminate fears or negative behavior.

STEPS IN HYPNOTHERAPY

People develop these tendencies because their self-image is
lowered as a result of unpleasant past experiences. Thus, the first
step in any form of hypnotherapy is to build up the patient's
self-image. This is done by the use of what we call "ego-
strengthening suggestions." For example, I might say to a patient
in a trance, "Every day, in every way, you are getting better, and
better, and better. Negative thoughts and negative suggestions
have absolutely no influence over you at any mind level."

In addition to adding to the patient's self-confidence, this
results in an increase in his or her motivation, concentration,
and energy levels. This is especially important when working with
people who are anxious or depressed.

The second step I follow is to systematically re-program the
subconscious so that the problem, once removed, will not occur
again. Eighty to ninety percent of cases of negative self-image can
be cured by the use of regression and progression. Through systematic re-programming suggestions, the problem can be eliminated
permanently. This is important because many people think that
removing a habit or phobia with the use of hypnosis will result

in substitution of a new habit or phobia. Nothing could be further from the truth.

At least 80 percent of the patients who request regression or progression do so with the objective of eliminating a habit or phobia or negative tendency. There are hypnotherapists who claim "one-shot cures" for smoking, overeating, and other bad habits, using hypnotic suggestion. A habit that has been programmed for many years into the subconscious mind requires more than one exposure to effect its permanent elimination. Also, the old technique of using aversion suggestion ("If you smoke a cigarette, you will get nauseous") never really worked and doesn't work today. Instead, all suggestions should be positively worded ("I am steadily losing my desire for a cigarette each and every day").

There are many other common fallacies and needless fears about hypnosis. To summarize:

1. The fallacy of symptom substitution. As I have mentioned, by using regression to see the true causes of a negative tendency and by using systematic re-programming suggestions to permanently eliminate the problem, symptoms are not substituted. They are permanently removed.

2. The fallacy of mind control. Earlier in this chapter I discussed the fact that absolutely nobody can be placed in a hypnotic trance against his or her will. Even a highly skilled hypnotherapist needs the cooperation of the patient in order to induce a trance. The only person capable of controlling a patient's subconscious mind is the patient.

3. The fallacy of revealing secrets or other information in trance. Unless the patient wants to reveal the information, the information in a patient's subconscious mind will remain hidden. Psychologists use the phrase "the ego cannot be detached" to describe this. For example, in a past life regression, if you saw yourself in an embarrassing or even humiliating scene, you would relive this scene in your mind but would not discuss it, even if you were in a very deep trance, unless you wanted to.

4. The fear of not being de-hypnotized. Because hypnosis is a natural process that the mind goes through each and

every day, and because we are constantly bringing ourselves into and out of trances, a patient can terminate a hypnotic trance any time that he or she wants to. Patients do not need a hypnotherapist to bring them out of a trance. I usually count from one to five to return the patient to the conscious state, but this is not necessary. The patient will resume conscious functioning by himself. However, counting forward facilitates this process.

5. The fear of not remembering suggestions afterwards. Unless you are a somnambule (capable of achieving a deep level trance), you will always remember the suggestions or scenes afterwards. I always give a post-hypnotic suggestion (a suggestion that is meant to work long after the trance ends) for the patient to remember everything they experienced or re-experienced upon awakening. The term "awakening" is a poor one, since the patient is not asleep, but most people can relate to this description.

The only time I do not suggest a patient remember what he or she has experienced in a trance is when I am working with someone who is emotionally upset and the scene is especially traumatic. If I don't feel that the patient can handle the information, then I will suggest that he forget it (hypno-amnesia). In any event, the information or scene will be remembered by the patient eventually as the post hypnotic suggestion wears off (approximately 4 to 10 days). Even somnambules will remember the scene if you give the appropriate post hypnotic suggestion.

6. The fear of regression. I know of no case where anyone has ever been harmed by the use of hypnosis in any form. I have done thousands of regressions and progressions and can personally testify to the many positive benefits. In all the time that I have used hypnosis, I have never seen or even heard of a negative effect or situation experienced by a patient. In my experience, the worst that can happen is nothing, i.e., no trance is induced.

Hypnosis is simply a way of relaxing and setting aside the conscious mind while at the same time activating the subconscious mind so that suggestions can be made directly to the subconscious, enabling the patient to act on these suggestions with greater ease and efficiency.

THE BENEFITS OF HYPNOSIS

From my double career as a dentist and a hypnotherapist, I have found two major therapeutic applications of hypnosis: first, past-life regression for the cure of unpleasant symptoms and negative behavior, and second, pain control. The second is an application which has been increasingly recognized by the Western medical community in recent years. Dentists and physicians are beginning to perform otherwise painful medical procedures using hypnosis instead of chemical anesthesia—with tremendous success.

I long ago postulated the idea of chemical mediators in hypnosis. Just as fear or excitement can cause the body, by way of the adrenal glands, to produce adrenalin (which acts to increase the heart rate and motivate a person toward quick and immediate action—so-called "fight or flight" mechanism), I felt that hypnosis might somehow stimulate the body to produce other types of chemical mediators. Recent research has proved this to be the case in the area of pain control.

Feeling pain consists of two processes. The first is the original pain signal that is transmitted to the brain from the point of stimulation, and the second is the interpretation of that signal by the brain. Hypnosis seems to alter the brain's interpretation of the pain signal by stimulating the brain's production of a chemical called *endorphin*.* Recent biochemical research has identified the chemical structure of endorphin as resembling that of morphine, except that it is ten times more potent than morphine, with none of morphine's addictive side effects. The brain also produces a chemical that destroys the effects of endorphin, so that the protective function of our pain-interpreting mechanisms can resume their normal functions.

Thus, current biochemistry has established the first link between hypnosis and an explanation of how it works. In the coming years, I expect many more chemical mediators in the

---

*Recent research has shown that endorphin cannot be the mechanism for hypnotic pain control since naloxene (a narcotic antagonist) doesn't reverse hypnoanalgesia.

brain to be discovered and analyzed to explain the many other positive actions and effects of hypnosis.

Below I've compiled a partial list of the many other benefits that hypnotherapy can be useful in achieving. Among these are:

1. increased relaxation and the elimination of tension
2. increased and focused concentration
3. improved memory ("hypernesia")
4. improved reflexes
5. increased self-confidence
6. pain control
7. improved sex life
8. increased organization and efficiency
9. increased motivation
10. improved interpersonal relationships
11. slowing down the aging process
12. harmony of the mind, body and spirit
13. elimination of habits, phobias and other negative tendencies
14. improved psychic awareness—ESP, meditation, astral projection (out of body experience), telepathy
15. elimination of the fear of death by viewing one's past and future lives.

I hope this chapter has helped make you aware of at least the basics behind hypnotherapy and its uses in regression and progression. Throughout the rest of this book I will be referring to the principles that have just been discussed.

Before one can truly benefit from actual case histories, a background on karma is necessary. In the next chapter I will explain what karma is and how the mechanisms of past and future lives work.

CHAPTER THREE

WHAT IS KARMA?
HISTORICAL FOUNDATIONS AND
POPULAR CONCEPTS

The purpose of my discussion of karma, reincarnation, progression, or any other aspect of parapsychology is to inform you of a very exciting field. It is not my intention to try to convert anyone to my beliefs nor do I want to state dogmatically that there is only one answer to the question of rebirth. In my work as a hypnotherapist, I have learned to keep an open mind. My concepts and opinions have changed through the years and will change again as new ideas and theories develop. This book and the knowledge it contains is an expression of my background, personality, interests, and experiences.

Karma is simply cause and effect. If you throw a rock through a window, putting a hole in the window, you have a cause (throwing the rock) and an effect (a hole in the window). Every effect that exists has some cause. If you are unhappy about your life, your financial situation, your relationships, your health, etc., then you must realize that causes exist. These causes can be traced back to past lives. Your subconscious mind retains all of these causes because it has a perfect memory bank. The subconscious mind also survives death, so that a new life is merely exchanging one body for another. You have the same subconscious, only now it has learned some lessons and grown spiritually.

All of the things you have or have not done in this and all of your past lives will generate certain effects in this life as well as in future lifetimes. The laws of karma are perfectly just. The soul always has free will. Karma can bring you happiness or sadness depending upon the causes you have earned, and the paths you have chosen to take. It is not the purpose of karma to reward or punish. Its purpose is to educate the subconscious, to purify it. Once the subconscious is purified, it no longer needs karma, or the "karmic cycle," as we refer to it. The karmic cycle is the chain of lives we live to work out all of the negativity we have earned in previous lifetimes.

The balance sheet or final result of the karmic cycle is zero. When all of the positive causes we've earned cancel out all of the negative causes, and we have learned all of the lessons that we are supposed to learn, then we have completed our karmic cycle. The balance sheet is zero and the subconscious is purified. We then no longer need to come back again to learn.

If, however, we react to certain tests in our lives negatively (with hatred, revenge, jealousy, pettiness, or some other negative emotion), then we have not learned our lesson but have failed the test and will have to retake this test in either this or a future lifetime.

KARMA—AN EASTERN TRADITION WITH A WESTERN APPLICATION

The belief in the pre-existence of an individual soul (or subconscious) has been called by many names. The terms *metempsychosis, transmigration, reincarnation, rebirth,* and *reembodiment* have been used to describe this mechanism. *Karma* is a Sanskrit word that literally means "action." (Sanskrit is an ancient Indo-European written language, dating from about 1500 B.C.) Karma is the force that leads to reincarnation. *Destiny* is another synonym for karma. In any one life we plant the seeds of the personality that will grow during that and subsequent incarnations (lifetimes). Thus, reincarnation is the mechanism by which karma works. The two must be considered together.

The basic Law of Karma has come to mean action and reaction, or cause and effect. This is equivalent to the Christian philosophy: "as ye do unto others, so shall it be done unto you." Any action that is considered harmful or evil to the well-being of another is punished exactly in proportion to the harm done.

One of the basic principles of karma is that every soul (entity) has free will. There is always freedom of choice. Each soul is drawn to parents who can provide the biological heredity and physical environment needed to learn karmic lessons. Psychic genetics is more important than biological genetics in determining the character of our lives. In addition, all lessons and deeds are recorded in the entity's Akashic records, which are used to determine each new lifetime. These records are the sum total of our past, present and future lives and are stored in our subconscious.

A Law of Retribution extends over the entire karmic cycle. This law allows an entity to enjoy, in one lifetime, what it has earned in previous incarnations.

Often people will say that they are incapable of doing something because of their karma. In this case karma is being used as a crutch. Karma neither rewards nor punishes. This universal law of cause and effect gives meaning to all actions. Nothing happens by chance. It is only through ignorance and misuse that karma results in destruction, pain, sorrow and suffering.

The concept of *transmigration* is included in Eastern karmic thought. Transmigration is the passage of the human soul from the mineral kingdom to lower animals and finally to man. Many Eastern philosophers reject this concept, as do the majority of Western karmic followers. Even those who do accept transmigration feel that it is impossible to revert back to the lower animal form once human form is achieved. I personally do not accept transmigration.

Every culture since ancient times has accepted the idea of karma in some form or other. I will now trace the origin of karma from the East to the West. Then I will present some current popular explanations of the phenomenon.

EASTERN KARMA

Hinduism

The Hindus called the soul Atman, which survives many lifetimes until it accomplishes its destiny of perfection, enlightenment and joy and finally attains direct insight into its identity with Brahman, the World Spirit, and thus eliminates the necessity of rebirth. Krishna states in the *Bhagavad-Gita*, the ancient Hindu script,

"Man doth not perish here or hereafter. The man dwells for an immensity of years and is then born again on Earth. Being thus born again he comes in contact with the knowledge which belonged to him in his former body and from that time he struggles more diligently to perfection.''

The Laws of Manu, Book V states:

"On the departure of the individual soul from this body and its new birth in another womb, and on its wanderings through ten thousand millions of existences.

On the infliction of pain on embodied spirits, which is caused by demerit, and the gain of eternal bliss, which is caused by the attainment of their highest aim through spiritual merit.''

Tibetian Buddhism

The "skandhas" (bundles of attributes or elements of limited existence) play a most important part in the transmission of "unfinished business" in Buddhist philosophy. These karmic connections between lives (skandhas) are similar in function to the DNA which makes up the chromosomes responsible for inherited characteristics in the physical body. These skandhas remain at death as karmic remnants and attach themselves to the subconscious and subsequently are reincarnated along with the subconscious.

The *Tibetan Book of the Dead*, written thousands of years ago by advanced yogis, describes the different types of experiences a soul (subconscious) will have after death. According to this text, a soul passes through many nonphysical worlds before coming back to earth to be reincarnated. The amount of time spent in each of these worlds depends entirely on one's state of spiritual development.

A soul may linger in its former environment on Earth and visit familiar places of its past, or just observe its previous body before entering one of the nonphysical worlds. Eventually the soul enters a world of souls where it re-evaluates its last lifetime and, after a certain period of time, is reborn into a new body.

One striking difference between the Hindus and the Buddhists in their concept of karma, is that the former believe in a permanent soul, whereas the latter maintain that everything in the universe is in a state of change. Buddhists consider the soul to be a conglomeration of habit patterns, attachments and instincts which are all subject to change. Thus, Buddhists feel that there is no permanent soul, just a pulsating subconscious which goes from lifetime to lifetime learning lessons until it achieves its liberation by attaining perfection. Buddhists say that the existence of the three "fires" of craving, ill-will and ignorance bring about rebirth. The extinction of these "fires" is symbolized by the word *Nirvana*, meaning "perfection."

Zoroastrianism

The teachings of Zoroaster of ancient Persia are preserved today by the Parsis of India. Mezoam separated man from the other animals by the presence of a soul. This soul is free and without a body or anything material. It is through the soul that man reaches God. Jam-i-Kaikhoshra stated, "After leaving this body a virtuous man acquires a still better place and body and his wisdom constantly increaseth."

The Koran

Under Islamic influence, Spain was a great center of philosophy. Avicebron, a Spanish Jew, brought the long forgotten teachings of Plato—who believed in a soul—back to European thought. During the Dark Ages in Europe, when the knowledge of Greece and Rome was all but lost, the doctrine of rebirth was being taught in the East by Al Ghazali and Al Batagni in the Schools of Bagdad. However, the Sufis, a Mohammedan mystical sect of Persia, did the most to preserve reincarnational thought in the East. The Sufis claimed to possess the esoteric philosophy of Islam. Saadi, Rumi, and Hafiz were Sufis Persian poets. A quote from the Koran, the sacred text of Islam, illustrates karma: "God generates beings, and sends them back over and over again, till they return to Him."

WESTERN KARMA

Stone-Age Karma

Primitive civilizations have often included human sacrifice as part of their rituals. They believed that only the body and not the soul was being sacrificed. Some North American and Central American Indians felt that human sacrifice helped the individual's karmic cycle.

In Great Britain, the ancient Celtic religion of witchcraft, or Wicca, was eventually replaced by the incorporation of reincarnation into their religious beliefs. This also applied to France and Scandinavia.

Egypt

According to Egyptian beliefs, transmigration was the accepted mechanism of reincarnation. After a person died, he would reincarnate as an animal for as long as 3000 years until his soul became purified. Only then could this soul return to the human form. The Books of Hermes states, "From one soul of the Universe are all Souls derived . . . of these Souls there are many changes, some into a more fortunate estate, and some quite contrary. The Soul passeth from form to form; and the mansions of her pilgrimage are manifold."

Greece

Orpheus was the founder of Greek theology. He taught the Greeks various sacred rites. Plato and Pythagoras used Orpheus as a source for their own philosophies.

In the *Life of Pythagoras* by Diogenes Laertius we find Pythagoras reviewing his previous lifetimes. He states that he was Aethalides and then Euphorbus, who was wounded by Menelaus at the siege of Troy and died there. As Aethalides, Pythagoras (582–507 B.C.) received the memory of his soul's incarnations as a gift from Mercury (God of Wisdom).

Plato (427–347 B.C.) states in Phaedrus, "Every soul is immortal. All that is soul presides over all that is without soul and patrols all Heaven, now appearing in one form and now in another. Every man's soul has by the law of his birth been a spectator of eternal truth, or it would never have passed into this our mortal frame, yet still it is no easy matter for all to be reminded of their past by their present existence."

In Laws, Book X, Plato states, "Know that if you become worse you will go to the worse souls, or if better to the better, and in every succession of life and death you will do and suffer what like may fitly suffer at the hands of like."

Ancient Judaism

Josephus, the Hebrew historian, states that there were three sects of philosophy among the Jews. These were termed the Essenes, the Pharisees and the Sadducees. The Sadducees believed that the soul died when the body died but both the Essenes and the Pharisees believed in rebirth.

Philo Judaeus (20 B.C.–A.D. 54) says in DeSomniis, "The air is full of souls; those who are nearest to Earth descending to be tied to mortal bodies return to other bodies, desiring to live in them."

The Kabala is a sacred text supposedly representing the hidden wisdom behind the Hebrew scriptures. It was derived by the Rabbis of the Middle Ages from older doctrines. Reincarnation often appears in the Kabala and was further developed in Hasidism. According to these teachings, all human souls have a common origin from primordial man (Adam Kadmon). Parts of Adam's soul (nitzotzoth) form every individual soul. Adam's original sin brought higher and lower souls into confusion. As a result, every soul had to pass through a series of incarnations before returning to God.

The ancient Jews believed that Moses was the reincarnation of Abel, the son of Adam. Their Messiah was to be the reincarnation of Adam himself, who had already come a second time as David.

Rome

The poet Ennius introduced karma to the Romans. In his *Annals*, Ennius tells how Homer appeared to him in a dream and told him that their bodies had the same soul. Virgil (70–19 B.C.) in the *Aeneid* says, "All these souls, after they have passed away a thousand years, are summoned by the divine ones in a great array, to the Lethean river. In this way they become forgetful of the former earthlife, and re-visit the vaulted realms of the world, willing to return again into living bodies."

Christianity

An early Christian philosopher by the name of Origen (A.D. 185–254), considered by some historians to be one of the most prominent of all of the Church Fathers, in his *Contra Celsum*, states, "Is it not more in conformity with reason that every soul for certain mysterious reasons is introduced into a body, and introduced according to its deserts and former actions? The soul, which is immaterial and invisible in its nature, exists in no material place without having a body suited to the nature of that place; accordingly, it at one time puts off one body, which was necessary before, but which is no longer adequate in its changed state, and it exchanges it for a second."

St. Augustine (A.D. 354–430), in *Contra Academicos*, discussed Plato's reincarnation by saying, "The message of Plato, the purest and most luminous in all philosophy, has at last scattered the darkness of error, and now shines forth mainly in Plotinus, a follower of Plato so like his master that one would think they lived together, or rather—since so long a period of time separates them—that Plato is born again in Plotinus."

There were many disputes over issues of Christian doctrine—especially over the preexistence of the soul—in the 500 years after the death of Christ. During the Dark Ages, the doctrine of reincarnation became hidden but fortunately did not disappear. Heretical Christian groups kept reincarnation and karma alive in the West.

In 529 A.D., Emperor Justinian closed the Neoplatonic School in Athens and banished the last of the Neoplatonists. For nearly a thousand years, with the exception of the Christian heretics, the concept of reincarnation disappeared from Christian Europe. Not until the 15th century in Florence, Italy, under the protection of the House of Medici, were the teachings of Plato and the concept of reincarnation revived.

George Gemistus (1355–1450) is credited with being the first person to reintroduce Plato to the Western world. Gemistus wrote, "As to ourselves, our soul remains immortal and eternal . . . attached to a mortal envelope, it is sent by the gods now into one body, now into another, in order that the union of the mortal and immortal elements in human nature may contribute to the unity of the whole."

Theosophy in the United States

In the last quarter of the 19th century, the Theosophical Society was founded in New York City by Mme. H. P. Blavatsky, Col.

H. S. Olcott, William Q. Judge, and others. It marked the first widespread movement in the modern Western world to investigate and study reincarnation and related concepts. This represented a synthesis of religion, philosophy, science and psychology.

Reincarnation in the East was thought of as a means to escape as quickly as possible from the wheel of rebirth and to attain Nirvana. Westerners considered the return to earth life as a penance or as a means of purging oneself of impurities. Theosophists regarded reincarnation as the universal law of evolutionary progress, holding that in an infinite universe there must be infinite possibilities for growth and development. Thus, one would never outgrow the need for new cycles of rebirth.

H. P. Blavatsky (1831–1891) expressed her views by stating, "The doctrine of Metempsychosis (reincarnation) has been abundantly ridiculed by men of science and rejected by theologians, yet if it had been properly understood in its application to the indestructibility of matter and the immortality of spirit, it would have been perceived that it is a sublime conception."

SUMMARIZING REINCARNATION AND KARMA

Karma means "action" or "reaction." Another way to define it is to state it simply as cause and effect. Christians say, "Do unto others as it should be done unto you." The Christian philosophy views this cause and effect as occurring during a single lifetime. Followers of karma and reincarnation carry it over from lifetime to lifetime.

The Law of Karma states that any single entity is born into a particular lifetime under the exact set of circumstances and with the exact set of capabilities to best utilize his or her karmic cycle. These qualities were the result of previous incarnations.

The Law of Retribution encompasses the entire karmic cycle. Thus the soul may benefit or suffer in one lifetime from the events of its previous lifetimes.

The Law of Karma has many advantages for its students. It offers an understanding of the frustrations and obstacles that are experienced by people who don't seem to deserve this environment. Second, it offers a more scientific explanation for the teachings of Christ and all other religious leaders. Third, it acts as a deterrent to selfish, thoughtless and harmful actions. Fourth, it facilitates the belief in an orderly universe, one in which law and order and a sense of moral purpose dominate.

One of the very attractive qualities about reincarnation and karma is the opportunity to meet challenges in new lives and to have a great deal of control over one's destiny. You might consider it a concept of evolution based on the laws of cause and effect. "As you sow, so shall you reap."

SOME POPULAR EXPLANATIONS OF KARMA AND THEIR BASIC PRINCIPLES

Below are some of the more popular concepts that attempt to explain karma and their major principles. I will not list every concept, because there seem to be more concepts than regressive hypnotherapists, but I will describe the most logical (in my opinion) and popular ones.

Before I do this, let me caution you about cults. During the past ten years, many cults, or pseudoreligions, as I call them, have surfaced and tried to sell their philosophies to unsuspecting Americans. If you allow anyone to control your thinking there will undoubtedly be negative karma generated as a result of this experience. The rule of thumb that I use whenever an organization presents itself with the "answers" to all of man's problems, and especially if a single leader is offered who will show you "the way," then that group is a cult.

The answers to one's karmic cycle lie within one's subconscious. Any human being who immodestly takes credit for your accomplishments either has an ego problem or a great misconception of karma or both. Shakespeare said it best when he wrote, "To thine own self be true."

Here are the concepts as promised.

The Plane Concept

According to the plane concept, our karmic cycle is worked out on five lower planes. On each of these lower planes an entity (soul) has a level of awareness or vibrational rate. In order to go to a higher plane, your vibrational rate must have reached a certain level. Each successive plane requires a higher vibrational rate. If it is not at this level, then the entity will go to that plane which best fits its level.

The Lower Five Planes:

1. *The earth plane or physical plane.* This is the plane that we function in now. The body is most material or physical at this level. The greatest amount of karma can be erased or added on at this level. This is by far the most difficult level.

2. *The astral plane.* The body is less material here. This is where the subconscious, or soul, goes immediately following death or crossing over. Ghosts are examples of astral bodies.

3. *The causal plane.* The body is even less material at this level. The Akashic records are kept here. This is where a medium projects him or herself when he or she reads your past or future.

4. *The mental plane.* This is the plane of pure intellect.

5. *The etheric plane.* The body is least material at this level. On this plane truth and beauty are most important.

The amount of time spent on these lower planes will depend entirely on the soul's achievements and remaining karmic debts. If you must develop intellectually then you would select the mental plane. If truth is most important to your karmic cycle then the etheric plane would be your choice. The earth plane represents the plane of greatest elimination of or addition to our karmic debts.

The Moment of Death

From the moment of death, the entity is placed in a very precarious position. This is a transition or adjustment period. We must first be made aware of the fact that we have died. This is accomplished by the very helpful guidance from highly evolved entities called Masters and Guides. These Masters and Guides have completed their karmic cycles many centuries ago. Their main purpose is to help us adjust to the fact that we have died and to lead us to the white light that will take us to the soul plane, where we will evaluate the last life and choose the next one. At this time, we may also see and communicate by telepathy with friends or relatives that have previously died. These entities will also try to persuade us to enter the white light.

If you don't enter the white light, you will remain on the astral plane as a troubled spirit. Most recently departed entities will find comfort in the last surrounding they inhabited on the earth plane. Thus, they will stay around their house or apartment. Some of their family may be made aware of their presence and they would interpret this as a ghost haunting their house. Indeed, many cases of haunted houses are explained in this fashion.

The Soul Plane

Eventually you will enter the white light and your destination will be the soul plane. Upon arriving at the soul plane you will be greeted by special guides who are assigned specifically to you for the purpose of orientation. Your guides will spend as much time as necessary to explain the nature of reality to you and your present purpose on this plane. You will be shown in detail the events from your last life and how they fit into your karmic patterns. Also, you will be shown scenes from past and future lives and your purpose will be to study these events in detail. It is as if you were a football player studying films of the team that you were scheduled to play that Sunday. Instead of preparing for a football game, you are preparing to choose your next life.

You are given a tremendous amount of help and advice by your Masters and Guides in these all-important decisions. First, you will have to select an era of time for your next life.

The historical time period that you choose is of great importance. Those of us here in the twentieth century are supposed to have been around during the days of Atlantis. I have regressed many patients back to the days of Atlantis (a highly advanced civilization probably located in the Bermuda Triangle) and Lemuria (a highly advanced civilization theorized to have been in the Pacific Ocean, and pre-dating Atlantis—50,000 B.C.)— both of which are now lost to us in the present. There are certain lessons that can best be learned during more primitive historical eras, such as the Dark Ages. The beginning of the Industrial Revolution would offer a stage for quite different challenges. Finally, the twentieth century, with nuclear power, space shuttles, laser beams, and other technological achievements, offers quite a different arena for our karmic lessons.

The length of time between lives varies greatly. When I regress patients back to the Middle Ages, it can be centuries in between lives. Regressions to the 18th and 19th centuries usually result in about 75 years from the end of one life to the beginning of the next. Twentieth-century regressions are the fastest in that there seems to be a range of from one year to twenty-five years between lives. Apparently, our vibrational rates and karmic lessons to learn are such that coming back rapidly is necessary in this century.

Astrology plays a major role in deciding a time period for your next life. The exact time, place, and date of birth will be very important. If you have artistic lessons to learn and sensitivity is to be experienced, then coming back as a Pisces would be indicated. Learning lessons as an executive or leader might dictate coming back as a Scorpio, Capricorn or Leo. Of course, your other planetary influences such as the moon, ascendent, Mars, Mercury, Venus, etc., must also be carefully selected.

In addition to astrology, "subcycles" must also be taken into consideration before any decision concerning the overall karmic cycle can be made. Within our karmic cycles, these smaller sub-cycles, such as certain emotional, intellectual, creative, and physical tasks, when completed, finish a certain phase within the total karmic cycle. Some parapsychologists say that every twelve lives makes up a sub-cycle. These twelve lives correspond to the zodiac signs in astrology. Theoretically, we choose a different astrological sign in each of these twelve lives to complete the cycle.

There is something called a "karmic chart" which can be constructed from your birth date, time and place. This is quite different from a regular astrological or natal chart in that it specifies what your sub-cycle is and can give you great insight into your overall karmic cycle.

On the soul plane, you will also be choosing your parents, brothers, sisters, and other family members, as well as planning all the major events in your life. These events must take into consideration the karmic cycle of these other people. Using the football analogy again, it would be like trying to formulate the schedule for the National Football League. Imagine how difficult it would be to formulate the schedule of so many teams, with conference, interconference, and other factors to consider to fulfill league requirements and at the same time try to make each team happy with its schedule.

Not only must you be fully aware of your own karmic cycle but you must be at least familiar with the karmic cycles of the many significant people that you will come into contact with in your new life. Whether you will be rich or poor, an only child or a member of a large family, black or white, weak or strong, will all depend on a very complicated selection process that your past life history will decide. Your Akashic records have all of this information and they will be your constant reference on the soul plane.

Akashic Records

These Akashic records are reportedly kept on the causal plane, but we do have access to them on the soul plane. They represent a file on the soul's growth and development throughout its many lives. They contain what the soul has learned and not learned. Thus, the soul's progression through its karmic cycle is what the Akashic records will show. By using these records we have intimate knowledge of what we have done and what we have to do. This is a most valuable aid.

For example, because of past karmic debts, in your next life you might need to stress the intellect. The emotional side of living would be underplayed so that the intellect could be developed to its maximum potential. Or the opposite situation might present itself. Your physical status is also important. A handicap, although it seems an obvious disadvantage in your new life, gives you the opportunity to learn certain lessons that would be difficult to learn if no such defect existed.

The Principle of Forgiveness

What is interesting to note about working out our karma is the principle of forgiveness. When I have the patient speak from the superconscious mind level I am informed of how this principle works. Assume that you lived during the time of the Vikings, about twelve hundred years ago. Raiding villages, burning buildings, raping the women and murdering the villagers would have been commonplace. This would incur much negative karma. If during one of these raids a certain group of villagers would have their lives spared because of your kindness, then you would earn positive karma. It wouldn't be just one positive episode against many negative ones. The fact that you showed this kindness would erase many negative episodes during that particular incarnation. If you spent the rest of that life helping other people, all of the past murders, thefts, and other crimes could be removed from your karmic cycle.

Free Will

Since the soul always has free will, it is our decision to be born at a certain time and place. It is our decision to choose our parents, friends, lovers, and enemies. We cannot blame other people or a bad childhood or marriage for our present problems. We are directly responsible for our lives because we have chosen the environment. The basic framework of your new life will be preplanned by you, but you can't plan every situation. Not only does *your* soul have free will, but so do *all* the souls that you will come into contact with in this new life. The main point here is that you choose the tests.

Group Karma

We do not just reincarnate individually. Rather, as I have been suggesting, our own separate karmic cycles are intertwined with many others. For example, your parents may have been your children in a former life. Your wife may have been your brother or son, etc. This is not to say that karma involves any form of incest or other such moral judgment. It simply implies the fact that our lessons are intermingled with the lessons of other entities. These lessons affect these two entities and others around them.

Group karma applies to everything we do. People who are killed in airplane crashes, wars, or other catastrophies actually chose that time and place to die. Case histories later in the book will develop this concept further.

Masters and Guides

We are aided in making these decisions by our Masters and Guides. These highly evolved entities have completed their karmic cycles and their purpose is simply to help and advise us as to our next lives. They do not moralize or pass judgment. They simply counsel us and try to help us as best they can. The individual soul always has free will to ignore their advice. Many of our decisions are poorly made for this very reason. These Masters and Guides also receive advice from even higher entities with higher vibrational rates in the seven higher planes. These much more advanced entities receive their advice from even more evolved sources, the ultimate authority being God or ALL THAT IS (as many parapsychologists refer to God). The final result is, of course, excellent guidance. When we listen to these guides, we make better decisions and work out our karmic cycles faster and with much less trauma.

Choosing a New Body

This is a very complicated process and group karmic considerations must be met. That is, you have to consider the karmic cycle of dozens of other entities before you can finalize your plans. These other entities must agree with your plans because they also have free will. This veto power can cause untold delays in the final framework of your and their next lives.

There can even be competition for certain bodies. Let's assume that you have completed your design of the basic framework for your next life. Now you must choose a newborn to enter. But let's say that another entity desires this same newborn for his or her karmic cycle and gets the right to inhabit it. You still have a karmic cycle to work out with the parents and other members of that newborn's family. You will now have to find another suitable newborn and devise a way to relate karmically to the parents and other family members of the newborn you were prevented from entering. We don't know exactly how the order on the waiting list for bodies is decided. It is probably based on a priority system giving those souls with the most important karmic lessons to learn first priority.

Once you have carefully chosen your next body and designed the basic framework of your next life, you are ready for the soul's entrance into the newborn. During the course of the pregnancy, each soul may visit its future body. Indeed, many souls actually enter the developing fetus, and this is why many people have prenatal memories that can be tapped through the use of hypnosis.

One reason that the soul can come and go as it pleases at this time is because the fetus' nervous system has not fully developed yet. There are openings in the skull (cranium) called "fontanelles" which allow the soul or subconscious to enter or leave the body. These openings will not close until the child is about 2½ years old. (Some people refer to these openings as a "chakra.") This helps explain the psychic nature of children.

The soul or subconscious actually enters the body of the newborn within 24 hours before or after the birth of the child. Many times during our childhood the soul will leave the body. This will occur during the waking hours as well as at night as the entity sleeps. All throughout our life the soul will leave the body during our sleep state, because it is during this sleep state that our Masters and Guides can continue teaching and advising us on our earthly progress. Thus, we are never really without the benefit of our guides, and the process of learning that began in between our lives never really ends.

Other Decisions on the Soul Plane

Much counsel is given to an entity on the soul plane. However, even with all this advice and plenty of time to make these decisions, some people choose to reincarnate before they are advised to. This is unfortunate because the necessary planning has not occurred. Instead of saving time, much time will be wasted and many errors will be made.

Relationships represent important decisions on the soul plane. Telepathic communication between you and the other entities involved will establish the details of who you will relate with and how in your next life. Your son in this life may be your father in your next life. Your wife or husband may be your brother or employer or parent.

Soul mates, or people with whom you have had very significant love relationships over many lifetimes, will be handled carefully. These soul mates represent the culmination of many lifetimes of being together and of sharing the most valuable emotion of all. You will not, however, be with your soul mates in every life.

In choosing your next life, the earth plane may not be to your liking. In that case you might choose any of the other lower planes (astral, causal, mental or etheric) to work out your karmic cycle. Life on these other planes isn't very different from that on the earth plane. People get married, have children, divorce, love, hate, etc. on all of the lower planes.

There are some entities that will not reincarnate immediately. They may act as teachers or a kind of guide themselves. Of course, only entities who are more highly evolved with higher vibrational rates will be able to take this karmic vacation. Eventually they too must come back and resume their karmic cycle.

The Seven Higher Planes

You may choose any of the lower five planes to work out your karma, but as long as you have a karmic cycle you cannot enter the seven higher planes—your vibrational rate would be too low to allow this to happen.

The lower five planes exist simultaneously but function at different frequencies. The frequencies are similar to a radio signal. Let's assume that the earth plane is at frequency 5000 and the astral plane is at frequency 5200. As long as your vibrational rate is 5000, you will not ascend to the astral plane.

Beyond the soul plane there are seven higher planes, with the highest plane being the nameless or God plane. On the God plane the essence of all of us resides. What this concept is saying is that God is within all of us, we are all creators and we create our own realities. God is also called ALL THAT IS by the followers of this concept. Thus, this God plane is the equivalent of Heaven.

What I find particularly appealing about this concept is that there is no Hell. Hell is merely the temporary negative aspects of one's lives on the lower five planes. However, there is a Heaven in this concept. Many people assume parapsychology to be an atheistic (no belief in God) or agnostic (not believing in God unless proof of its existence can be obtained) discipline, but nothing could be farther from the truth. When we reach the God plane we are perfect. The subconscious—or soul—is pure.

As with the lower five planes, it is your vibrational rate that determines which of the seven higher planes you enter. If your vibrational rate is for the eighth plane, then that is where you would reside. Your level of consciousness—your thoughts and actions—determines your vibrational rate.

The plane concept can best be illustrated by the following diagram:

	GOD OR NAMELESS PLANE (PLANE 13)	
SEVEN	PLANE 12	
HIGHER	PLANE 11	
PLANES	PLANE 10	
	PLANE 9	
	PLANE 8	
	PLANE 7	
	SOUL PLANE (PLANE 6)	
KARMIC	ETHERIC PLANE (PLANE 5)	
CYCLE	MENTAL PLANE (PLANE 4)	
(LOWER 5	CAUSAL PLANE (PLANE 3)	AKASHIC RECORDS
PLANES)	ASTRAL PLANE (PLANE 2)	
	EARTH PLANE (PLANE 1)	*YOU ARE HERE*

FIGURE 2

SOME OTHER POPULAR CONCEPTS OF KARMA

The Oversoul Concept

This particular karmic concept claims that you are part of a larger soul. You are merely an extension of this complete soul. In order for this oversoul to learn many different lessons, it creates smaller souls so that it is living many lives simultaneously. Past, present, and future occur simultaneously, according to this concept.

One interpretation of this concept places the oversoul on the God plane. Thus, although we are functioning on the lower planes, we are all directly part of God. We would then all be Gods.

Some regressions have uncovered parallel lives or one entity reporting two former lives at the same dates but in different locations, lending credence to this view.

Simultaneous Multiple Incarnation Concept

As the earth's frequency begins to accelerate with technological advancements, more and more of the older souls will now be attracted to coming back to this era of time. These very mature souls have the ability to inhabit many bodies at one time. Thus, they can speed up our evolutionary process.

Also, many parapsychologists feel that only highly evolved souls with certain vibrational rates would be able to survive in the Twentieth Century.

The Space-Time Continuum

This concept states that there is no such thing as the past, present, or future as we know it. All of our lives are being lived at the same moment but at different frequencies. Thus, your past lives are occurring right now on a different frequency along with your present and future lives. They are all affecting each other. You are thus able to change the past and future by changing the present.

To illustrate this concept, imagine yourself in a space ship leaving the Earth. As you look back down on the Earth you see the present occurring in Europe, the past in South America and the future in North America. As you return to the Earth you choose which era, or continent, by this example, you want to function in. Einstein's Theory of Relativity, which tells us that there is only the probability—not the certainty—of the existence of matter at any point in time, is in line with this concept.

PAST   PRESENT   FUTURE

FIGURE 3

The Linear Concept of Reincarnation

This concept simply states that the past is history, the present is occurring now and the future hasn't occurred yet. This is the notion of time we are most familiar with. Thus, your past and future lives have no direct effect on your present life, and vice versa. This is, of course, in conflict with the classical concept of karma, on which this book is based.

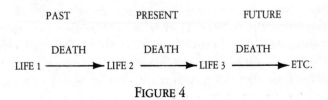

PAST   PRESENT   FUTURE

DEATH   DEATH   DEATH

LIFE 1 ———→ LIFE 2 ———→ LIFE 3 ———→ ETC.

FIGURE 4

The Extraterrestrial Concept

This concept assumes that sometime between 100,000 B.C. and 50,000 B.C. the Earth was visited by beings from another planet. Their purpose was to observe the Earth. These beings were pure energy and had no bodies, as we know them. They were curious about what it would be like to have a body, so they took over the body of man at that time. These extraterrestrials were able to leave the body at any time. However, because they misused the body and committed all kinds of negative acts, they were punished by being trapped inside the body. Their own karma was pre-established, and all they had to do was work out this minimal karmic debt and they would be free to leave the body upon its death. However, their karma was increased by further negative actions and thus we have our current karmic cycle.

This concept offers some interesting explanations. Our immediate predecessors (Cro-Magnon man) lived from about 40,000 B.C. to about 25,000 B.C. Neanderthal man preceded Cro-Magnon man and lived from about 75,000 B.C. to about 40,000 B.C.—during the time the extra-terrestrials are said to have come to earth. One interesting note about the evolution of modern man (*homo sapiens*) is that we evolved far faster than we should have. Evolution is a very slow process, yet the difference between Cro-Magnon man and modern man is enormous. Since I don't believe in coincidence or mere chance, it is obvious that some other factors were at work in our evolution. A possible explanation for this rapid evolution is that these extraterrestrials, by means of some form of genetic engineering, altered the makeup of Neanderthal and Cro-Magnon's brain cells to allow more intelligent thought patterns to be exhibited.

The ancient civilizations of Atlantis (in the Atlantic Ocean) and Lemuria (in the Pacific Ocean) were said to have begun between 75,000 B.C. and 50,000 B.C. There have been many books published suggesting the physical evidence of visitors from other planets. If the idea interests you, by all means pursue it.

I have only attempted to sketch in some background data concerning karma. As far as your belief in a particular concept goes, you may choose from these or form your own opinion. Whatever you do, keep an open mind. When the student is ready the teacher will be there. If you don't believe in karma or reincarnation, don't worry. You probably will in your next life.

CHAPTER 4

DOCUMENTED PROOF OF REINCARNATION

Is it possible to prove the concept of reincarnation beyond any shadow of doubt? The answer must be no, with the present limitations of our available data. Even with all of the documented cases, no matter how many facets of a case check out, there will always be skeptics who will try to explain the results by coincidence or some other outdated answer.

It is physically impossible to determine just how much of what a patient has read or been exposed to is mistakenly reported as the impression of a past life during hypnotherapy. Still, when a child reports information in a regression using the vocabulary of an adult or speaks in foreign languages which he or she has never been exposed to, I find no other explanation more plausible than reincarnation.

In this chapter I will present just a few of the best documented cases of reincarnation. These should make some of the skeptics think twice.

BRIDEY MURPHY—FACT OR FICTION

The Bridey Murphy story is not the first documented case of a previous lifetime, but it is by far the best known. Morey Bernstein, a businessman in Pueblo, Colorado, regressed Mrs. Virginia Burns Tighe (called Ruth Simmons in the book) between November 29, 1952 and August 29, 1953. Mrs. Tighe's past life was in Belfast, Ireland in the 1800's and her name was Bridey Murphy. The results of these six tape recorded hypnotic regressions were published in 1956 by Doubleday and Company as *The Search For Bridey Murphy*.

Morey Bernstein had learned to use hypnosis and for ten years prior to his regressing Mrs. Tighe, he had offered his services as a hypnotist without charge to local physicians. At first Mr. Bernstein was very skeptical about the idea of past life regression. As the sessions continued, he became convinced that Mrs. Tighe had, in fact, lived before.

In 1952 Virginia Tighe was married. She and her husband were only casually acquainted with the Bernsteins. Mrs. Tighe was born in 1923 and lived in Madison, Wisconsin until she was three years old. At that time she moved to Chicago, where she grew up. After attending Northwestern University for a year and a half, she married an Army Air Corpsman who was killed in World War II in 1944. After moving to Denver, she married businessman Hugh Brian Tighe and raised three children in Pueblo, Colorado.

Morey Bernstein chose Mrs. Tighe as his subject because he had hypnotized her twice before and realized that she was capable of achieving a very deep hypnotic trance. She also knew nothing of Morey's interest in reincarnation. Neither Bernstein nor Virginia Tighe had ever travelled to Ireland.

In trance, Mrs. Tighe described her life in Ireland. She was born in Cork in 1798, the daughter of a barrister named Duncan Murphy and his wife Kathleen. Virginia's name in this life was Bridey Murphy and she had a brother named Duncan Blaine Murphy. Bridey attended a school run by a Mrs. Strayne. Duncan eventually married Mrs. Strayne's daughter Aimee. Bridey had a second brother who died as a baby. She was Protestant, and at age twenty married Sean Brian Joseph McCarthy, the Catholic son of a Cork barrister. The young couple later moved to Belfast where Brian attended law school and taught law at Queen's University. There had been no children during their life together. In 1864 Bridey died at the age of sixty-six.

There were many attempts to prove and disprove the accounts of Mrs. Tighe's six regressions. I will discuss only those facts that were verified and which leave little doubt as to the authenticity of this case.

Bridey mentioned Farr's and John Carrigan as two Belfast grocers from whom she bought food. John Bebbington, the chief librarian in Belfast, verified this fact. In addition, these two men were the only individuals of those names that were in the food-stuff business in Belfast at that time. Bridey also mentioned a rope company and a tobacco house that were operating in Belfast. These also have been verified.

Some of the statements that Bridey made were refuted by experts based on known facts but were later shown to be correct after all. An example of this is the statement by Bridey that as a child she received a spanking for scratching all of the paint off her metal bed. Experts reported that iron beds were not introduced into Ireland until at least 1850. The Encyclopedia Britannica stated that iron beds appeared in Ireland in the eighteenth century.

Second, Bridey called the place in which she lived "the Meadows." A map of Cork in 1801 showed an area named Mardlike Meadows, where about half a dozen houses were indicated. Third, she stated that her husband taught law at the Queen's University in Belfast in 1847. Experts said that Queen's College was not founded until 1849 and Queen's University wasn't established until 1908. Subsequent research found that on December 19, 1845, Queen Victoria declared that "there shall and may be erected . . . one college for students in arts, law, physics . . . which shall be called Queen's College, Belfast." On August 15, 1850 Queen Victoria founded Queen's University in Ireland and stated "that the said Queen's Colleges shall be, and . . . are hereby constituted colleges of our said university."

Fourth, Bridey mentioned little sacks of rice which were tied to the leg as a sign of purity. *Life Magazine*'s expert on folklore, Richard Hayward, refuted this by saying that rice had never been part of Irish folk traditions. But rice was, in fact, imported into Ireland at about 1750. Since rice is white it would naturally suggest purity and this custom is quite possibly accurate.

Fifth, Bridey talked about reading a book called *The Sorrows of Deirdre*. Experts stated that according to the English catalogue of books published between 1800 and the present, the first appearance of this book was in 1905. Later it was discovered that an inexpensive paperback was published in 1808 by Bolton entitled *The Song of Deirdre and the Death of the Sons of Usnach*.

Sixth, she mentioned the use of tuppence as one of the coins used in her day. This proved to be correct but only very few people knew that this particular coin was in use in Ireland only from 1797 to 1850. There were many other rather obscure facts that were initially disputed by experts but were subsequently corroborated upon further investigation.

It is interesting to note that throughout these six recorded sessions, Bridey gossiped and exaggerated her actual position in life. It soon became obvious that she was a member of the lower class (probably a coachman's wife or the wife of a messenger for a barrister). Her attempts to raise herself to the middle class and the awe and jealousy that she exhibited toward the middle class are natural responses. However, these qualities would hardly have been presented as such if this were all a hoax.

One final note on this case is the session centering on the last years of Bridey's life in Belfast. Mrs. Tighe spoke with a weary, half-whine and a throaty Irish accent that defies all explanation other than reincarnation. She could hardly have been exposed to it in this life, since the accent of the Belfast slums has never been used by American actors. Also, to have mastered such an accent, Mrs. Tighe would have had to be a very accomplished actress. As a "typical American housewife," she possessed none of these qualities. In my opinion, these last tapes illustrating this accent are more convincing of her life as Bridey Murphy than many of the controversial facts she stated that have subsequently been verified.

THE RESEARCH OF DR. IAN STEVENSON

Dr. Ian Stevenson was born in Montreal, Canada on October 31, 1918. He received his medical training at McGill University and was later associated with the Alton Ochsner Medical Foundation of New Orleans and Cornell Medical College. From 1949 to 1957 Dr. Stevenson was assistant and associate professor of Psychiatry at the Louisiana State University School of Medicine. From 1957 to 1967 he was chairman of neurology and psychiatry at the University of Virginia Medical School. Since then he has been alumni professor in psychiatry.

Much of Dr. Stevenson's research has been in reincarnation. His book entitled *Twenty Cases Suggestive of Reincarnation* deals with interviews of children whose memories very strongly suggested reincarnation. Dr. Stevenson is recognized as one of the world's foremost authorities on reincarnation.

The case of a five-year-old Lebanese boy named Imad Elawar, who in 1964 lived in the village of Kornayal, provides an interesting example of documented reincarnation. Imad claimed to have been in his last life Ibrahim Bouhanzy, who died of tuberculosis on September 8, 1944 at the age of 25. After eliminating the possibility of the child receiving information of this family from travelers or other family members, Dr. Stevenson questioned Imad about his past life. Imad claimed to recall his former family and the place where he had lived. He mentioned the names Mahmoud and Jamile (whom he described as beautiful, well-dressed and wearing a red dress that he had given her). A sister named Huda was mentioned along with Amin, Mehibe, Adil, Talil, Toufic, Salim, Kamel and Said, whom he referred to as brothers.

A total of fifty-seven claims had been made; fifty-one proved to be correct. Imad did not visit the village of Khriby of his former life until Dr. Stevenson came onto the scene. Jamile, it seems, had been Ibrahim's mistress. When Imad was four, he rushed up to a stranger and hugged him. Imad stated that they were neighbors. The stranger had, in fact, lived in Khriby and had been a neighbor of Ibrahim Bouhamzy.

Dr. J. G. Pratt, an associate of Dr. Stevenson's at the University of Virginia Medical School, aided Dr. Stevenson in his analysis of this most remarkable case. They both concluded that it was not practically possible for Imad to have travelled to Khriby, due to the topography. Fraud was also dismissed after a careful analysis was made of the evidence collected. Neither family stood to gain and both stood to lose by lying.

Another interesting case is William George. George was a Tlingits Indian fisherman in Alaska who at the age of sixty (in 1949) told his son and daughter-in-law that he would return as their son. He stated that they would recognize him by his present birthmarks, and he gave them a gold watch to hold for him. William George disappeared while fishing shortly afterwards. Less than a year later his daughter-in-law had a son who had the exact same birthmarks as William George.

As the boy grew up, he mimicked his grandfather in many ways, including a limp which William George had incurred in a basketball game. The boy also correctly identified the gold watch by picking it out of his mother's jewelry box unprompted. He also constantly referred to his uncles as "sons" and his great-aunt as "sister."

Dr. Stevenson wrote: "He shows a precocious knowledge of fishing and boats. He also shows greater than average fear of water for boys of his age. He is more grave and sensible than other children of his group."

A PSYCHIATRIST EXPLORES HIS OWN PAST LIFE

Dr. Arthur Guirdham, an eminent British psychiatrist, stated in 1977 that he and one of his patients shared a past life together and that he was convinced that reincarnation was a fact.

In 1962 a patient called Mrs. Smith came to see Dr. Guirdham about nightmares that she had been having. These scenes always involved her lying on a floor in a room awaiting some terrible event. Soon after seeing Dr. Guirdham the nightmares stopped but memories of a past life emerged.

She reported a life as a member of the Cathar sect, a persecuted religious cult in thirteenth century France. Mrs. Smith stated that Dr. Guirdham was her lover, that his name was Rogiet, and he was a blue-robed priest of the Cathars.

Dr. Guirdham contacted a noted French historian, Professor René Nelli, and asked him to investigate this matter. Professor Nelli is on the faculty at Toulouse University in France and he is an authority on thirteenth century French history. Each fact that Dr. Guirdham provided Professor Nelli from Mrs. Smith's visions checked out.

The clinching item seemed to be the blue robes of the Cathar priests. Scholars had for centuries maintained that these robes were black. Professor Nelli's research proved Mrs. Smith correct and the scholars incorrect. No history book contained this information. Only ancient records written in a language that Mrs. Smith had no knowledge of contained this all-important information. Mrs. Smith could not possibly have known about the blue robes beforehand.

THE CASE OF JONATHAN POWELL

When George Field was fifteen years old and living in Hinsdale, New Hampshire, he was hypnotized by the late Loring G. Williams into a past life as Jonathan Powell. George stated that his father's name was William Powell and his paternal grandmother was Mary Powell. They were Quakers who lived in the village of Jefferson in Ashe County, North Carolina. Their house was near the "Big Hill."

During the Civil War Jonathan had to work for the Northern army soldiers. He hated those "damn Yankee soldiers." One day, when he refused to sell five sacks of potatoes to these soldiers because they offered him such a low price, they shot him in the stomach and killed him.

Williams, George Field and a number of others drove down to Ashe County to verify this account. Powell was an uncommon name during that time in Ashe County. A local historian, Eleanor Baker Reeves, confirmed that a Jonathan Powell had actually lived.

After being regressed again George Field was asked questions by Ms. Reeves. She confirmed that George had an accurate knowledge of fifteen of the twenty people she asked him about. Well over 60 percent of the answers George gave to her questions were found to be correct. Field also exhibited great knowledge of the changes in the topography of Ashe County from 1860 to 1965.

George Field had never been to Ashe County before. He also described a river called South Fork, which did not show up on the maps of his home state (New Hampshire), but did show up on local North Carolina maps. Also, most of the residents of the village were Baptists but there were a few Quakers present.

A woman whose maiden name was Powell was located, and she claimed to be Jonathan Powell's great-grandniece. She stated that her great-granduncle was killed by Union soldiers during the Civil War, but she didn't know the details about his death.

Last, George Field spoke of Yankee soldiers wearing gray uniforms. Eleanor Reeves stated that even though Union soldiers normally wore blue uniforms, at that time there were bands of renegade soldiers who came from the North, wore gray uniforms and raided and plundered some Southern villages. Jonathan Powell could have easily been killed by one of these renegade soldiers.

THE CASE OF HENRIETTE WEISZ-ROOS

Henriette Roos was a portrait artist and concert pianist who lived in New York. She recalls that she was Rossaritta Weisz, a miniature portrait painter, in Bordeaux, France during the 1820's. She also claims to have given asylum to the famous Spanish painter Goya when he was exiled from Spain.

Henriette showed great skill as an artist as a child in Holland, although she never had any formal training in art. She married a Hungarian pianist and composer named Franz Weisz at the age of seventeen.

After showing some of her work to the Royal Dutch Academy in Amsterdam, Henriette was enrolled there as a student and graduated with honors. She divorced Weisz soon after, but kept his name, contrary to the local custom, and was now called Henriette Weisz-Roos. She had a strange attraction to the name Weisz.

In the summer of 1936 in Paris, Henriette, unable to sleep, was compelled to paint in the dark. She did this for several hours and then went back to bed. When she awoke the next morning she discovered that she had painted a beautiful portrait of a young woman. It was the best work she had ever done. She contacted a medium and found out that Goya was repaying the kindness, which she had shown him by offering him asylum in 1820 in France, by guiding her art career.

Several days later, Henriette found a book about the life of Goya. She learned that a woman named Leocardia Weisz gave Goya asylum during his exile from Spain. Leocardia had a daughter named Rossaritta Weisz who was a miniature portrait painter and who looked after Goya. After reading this account, she dropped the name Weisz from her surname.

What is interesting to note is the following:

1. Both Henriette and Rossaritta were miniature portrait painters.

2. Both Henriette and Rossaritta were fond of cats.

3. Both Henriette and Rossaritta were sympathetic toward the poor.

4. Rossaritta was crushed to death in a crowd at the age of twenty-seven. Henriette was always afraid of crowds.

5. Henriette came from a family without any interest or background in painting, yet she showed natural talents in this field.

6. Henriette never made it public that she was directly inspired by Goya. Her silence showed that she never tried to profit from her past life, thus discounting the accusation of fraud.

7. Henriette's portrait style is very similar to that of Goya.

8. Henriette was unusually attracted to her married name of Weisz, and she violated a local custom in keeping that name for some time after her divorce.

EDGAR CAYCE

Edgar Cayce was an uneducated man who spent most of his life in Virginia Beach, Virginia. He is one of the world's best known psychics. His specialty was in diagnosing medical conditions of people he had never met. When placed in a hypnotic trance, Cayce would not only correctly diagnose the patient's medical problem but would recommend the correct treatment in approximately 99 percent of the cases he handled. He would receive a letter from someone he did not know, and just from the patient's name, would recite the diagnosis and prescription. Mr. Cayce had no conscious knowledge of medicine nor did he even believe in reincarnation until very late in his life.

At the time of his death in 1945 Edgar Cayce had given more than 14,000 telepathic-clairvoyant readings; 2,500 of these are called "life readings." These "life readings" traced the past lives of the individual and aided them greatly in understanding their present problems. These discourses have fortunately been preserved and are kept in the library of the Association For Research and Enlightenment at Virginia Beach. Each reading is carefully indexed and notes the name of the stenographer, the conductor of the session and all witnesses present. In addition, each reading is accompanied by background information, if there is any, along with follow-up correspondence with the individual, his doctor, or his family. I highly recommend reading the story of his life and other books that have been written about him.

XENOGLOSSY

Xenoglossy is the speaking and / or writing of a foreign language in trance by a person who possesses no conscious knowledge of this language. When children are regressed and speak or write foreign languages fluently, which they have not been exposed to in this life, I consider this proof of reincarnation. One could rationalize a word or phrase being mastered in a foreign language by a child, but not an entire language. There is no way that a person's subconscious mind could have been exposed to an entire foreign language without conscious awareness of this. When adults or children start writing in hieroglyphics or other dead languages, I start thinking about past lives.

The case histories that fill the bulk of this book are my own documented experiences with past and future lives. All the evidence has been collected during private sessions with my patients, and much of the dialogue is transcribed directly from tape recordings, made with my patients' full knowledge and permission.

The potential benefits from regression therapy are limitless as you shall shortly see. With the background you have acquired from these first four chapters you are now ready for a more detailed explanation about what regression is and how it works.

CHAPTER FIVE

ON A CLEAR DAY YOU CAN
SEE YESTERDAY: AGE
REGRESSION WITH HYPNOSIS

WHY DO PATIENTS SEEK PAST LIFE
REGRESSION HYPNOTHERAPY?

There are a multitude of experiences from past lives that can negatively affect us in our present daily lives. A fear of water can be the result of drowning in a past life. A woman who died in a desert sand storm when she was a nomad in her last life now has an unusual fear of wind.

Insomnia was treated in a middle-aged woman by revealing a previous lifetime as a male Civil War sentry for the South who fell asleep at her post. Union soldiers killed her (him in that life) and her fellow soldiers, so the karmic association of going to sleep and death was well established. Fortunately, reliving that lifetime removed the insomnia.

An overweight man starved to death in a past life. Another man wondered why he was such an overprotective father until he found out that he had deserted his family in two previous incarnations.

A teenage girl came to see me because she was afraid of meeting new people. In the 1700's she was a little girl confined to a hospital in France for three weeks. Every time she had a visitor, the nurse would wash her face very roughly, getting soap in her eyes and nose. It was not surprising to learn that in this life every time she met someone new her nose began to hurt.

A workaholic in this life witnessed his family starving to death in Greece hundreds of years ago because he was not able to adequately provide for them. By overworking himself in this life, he

56

was preventing that from ever happening again. Fortunately for him, his past life regressions removed his workaholic compulsions permanently.

A woman suffering from frigidity in this life found out that she was rejected by her husband in a past life because she was raped. Her husband in this life was the same entity as her husband in that past life. By being frigid, she was repaying him for his actions. Today, she is no longer frigid thanks to past life regression.

I personally feel that there isn't a problem or negative tendency that past life regression therapy cannot help. I also feel that this is the very best and most efficient form of therapy that has ever been devised. The case histories presented in this book are just a sample of the kinds of real life problems that can be helped with past life regression.

The most important benefit of regression and progression therapy is not the retelling of scenes from past or future lives. It is a change in perspectives on life, an enlightenment as to who you are and what you are supposed to be doing here. The realization of constant evolution to something bigger, better, and more fulfilling is very beautiful to witness. I witness this every week of my life.

AGE REGRESSION

Regression is simply going back in time. If you think about what you had for lunch yesterday, you are regressing with your conscious mind. Hypnotic regression is going back in time utilizing the subconscious mind with its perfect memory bank. I will use the term *simple age regression* to refer to going back in time in this lifetime. The term *past life regression* will refer to the going back in time in a prior lifetime.

Simple age regression is by no means a simple procedure. The patient is guided back in time by systematic disorientation as to the present year, month and day. Appropriate suggestions are then given to reach the earlier age. Personality traits characteristic of this age will often be exhibited by the regressed patient. For example, speech patterns, handwriting and other characteristics of that earlier age become evident.

There are two types of age regression. The first type is called *revivification*. In this type the hypnotized patient actually relives or re-experiences the events of his or her life at an earlier age. For the duration of the trance, all memories following the regressed age are removed. Only somnambules (patients capable of very deep trance) are capable of achieving this deep level trance. Although it is easier to obtain desired information at this level, it is not necessary to attain this level to use simple age regression.

The second type of age regression is called *pseudo-revivification*. This type is characterized by the patient being able to relive scenes from an earlier age, but the memories following this age are not forgotten. In other words, the patient is aware that he or she is still in the present but the scenes are from the past. Their speech, handwriting and other characteristics will not have changed from those they possess currently. This is by far the most common form of age regression and much detailed information can be obtained. In this type of regression, as with any type of regression, the patient will re-experience the emotions of the scenes he or she is reliving.

At no time is the patient in danger of being trapped in this earlier age. Even in true revivification the patient can come back to the present at any time he or she wants to.

One characteristic of both types of regression is *hypermnesia*, or heightened recall. The memory banks of the subconscious mind are now being tapped and the patient can recall literally anything that he or she has seen, heard, touched, smelled or tasted. As long as you physically experienced something, age regression can bring the information back. In fact, the use of hypnosis in criminal investigation has received much attention during the past ten years—for just the reason we have been discussing: the strength of recall under hypnosis. From remembering license plate numbers to recalling the details of a rape or murder case, hypnosis has been accepted as an important evidence-gathering technique by many police departments. The fact that courts have utilized the services of hypnotherapists shows the change in public opinion as to the validity of this technique.

Not long ago, I had occasion to use hypermnesia in a legal case. The patient, whom I shall refer to as Ralph, was involved in a car accident on New Year's Day in the early morning hours.

He was referred to me by a former hypnosis patient. Ralph, a very likable man in his late thirties, simply could not recall the details of what happened on that fateful morning. Since this was a legal case and since the details of the accident were crucial to determine insurance liabilities, my services were requested.

Ralph went to a New Year's Eve dance with his wife Susan and three other couples. At about 3:00 A.M. Ralph and Susan decided to go to a bar called Dunhills to wish Happy New Year to a friend of theirs who owned the bar. After parking their car on Calvert Street they walked across the street to Dunhills. As they crossed the street a large van hit Ralph and Ralph completely repressed (pushed the scene back into the subconscious) all knowledge of the actual accident itself. The next thing that he remembered was being in a hospital at about 5:00 A.M. that morning.

Nearly a year later, Ralph, Susan and their attorney came to my office for the initial session. At this time I explained what hypnosis was and wasn't and an initial trance was induced. The attorney was impressed with Ralph's relaxed state during the trance.

The second session was held on November 20th, but I was unable to obtain any information. Ralph came alone to this and the successive sessions. I was not surprised at this initial failure since I was attempting to re-explore a very traumatic event. Regression conditioning suggestions were given and he was dismissed. During the next two sessions, Ralph recalled scenes from December 26th through December 31st, but I was still unable to re-explore the moment of impact.

On December 15th the entire accident was relived and this session was recorded. I repeated the regression on December 22nd and also recorded the session. Here are some excerpts from this last session:

Dr. G.: Carefully, step by step, tell me what you experienced next.
Ralph: I felt something hit me.
Dr. G.: On what side did you feel something hit you?
Ralph: On my right side.
Dr. G.: Did you hear any noise before the impact?
Ralph: No.

Dr. G.:   Did you see what hit you?

Ralph: No. No, I was facing the other way, looking to my left.

Dr. G.:   What do you see at the moment of impact?

Ralph: I can see myself trying to catch my balance, but I'm falling and knocking Susan down.

Dr. G.:   When you are on the ground where is the vehicle that hit you?

Ralph: It, it is to my right.

Dr. G.:   Where are the wheels of this vehicle in relation to the central white line on Calvert Street?

Ralph: The right wheels of the van are on the Dunhills side side of the white line, but the left wheels are on the other side of the line.

Dr. G.:   How do you feel now?

Ralph: I hurt all over. I can barely move and all I can feel is constant pain.

Dr. G.:   Sleep now and rest and detach yourself from all discomforts. Focus now on my voice. When I reach the count of five you will awaken refreshed, relaxed and will recall everything you re-experienced. One, two, three, four, five, awaken.

As you can see, Ralph was able to provide much information as to the moment of impact and the events that followed.

The use of age regression in treating habits and phobias makes use of this re-experience effect to help the patient understand why he or she acquired a particular negative tendency and what emotions were felt at the time. This last point is particularly important because the repressed emotions seem to account for about 80 percent of the causes of a patient's problem. The repressed scene alone accounts for the remaining 20 percent. By using age regression, a patient can relive the visual memories along with the emotions, and by bringing up these repressed emotions, he or she is effecting the cure to the problem. Simple age regression can also be used to help recover lost items, especially if related to a traumatic event.

The reason we develop symptoms of headaches, backaches, arthritis, colitis, allergies, asthma and many others is because of a breakdown in our conscious mind's repression mechanism. If we experience a particularly negative scene along with unpleasant emotions, the conscious mind has a natural tendency to repress or bury these memories and emotions in the subconscious mind. However, with time this repression mechanism breaks down and the memories begin to surface. The surfacing of these memories without the emotions is too much for the conscious mind to take. It decides against dealing with this scene. In order to divert its attention, a negative physical symptom is created. By reliving the scene and re-experiencing the repressed emotions, many physical symptoms can be permanently removed.

PAST LIFE REGRESSION

The use of past life regression can eliminate the causes of other habits, phobias and negative tendencies. There are many techniques to regress a patient into a past life. Some therapists use simple age regression to go back to the birth experience and then suggest the next logical step—going back into a past life.

I don't feel this is necessary. For one thing, birth is a traumatic experience for everyone. Second, the subconscious mind knows all about your past lives and doesn't need a map to find them. I simply ask the patient's subconscious in trance to go back to the origin of a particular problem or to relive a prior life that would give insight and understanding to the patient's present life.

Many people are curious about what they will experience in a past life regression. There are many possible experiences. First, you may see a scene and at the same time be aware of information related to this scene. I refer to this as both an audio and visual experience and it results in excellent data. Fortunately, it is the most common experience with my patients. It's as if you are watching a movie or television show.

The second type of experience consists of seeing cloudy or quick impressions that tend to disappear just as you are about to understand them. Another reaction is appearing to ''know'' or be aware of the environment without actually seeing or hearing anything. Feeling as if someone were whispering in your ear is another possibility. Reading words that appear before your inner eyes is a very rare type of experience, although this may be how some people know what the date is or what country they are living in.

Although there are people who regress large groups of people into past lives, I am a believer in individual regressions. I have done both individual and group past life regressions and I have experienced much better detailed information with individuals. When I work with a patient individually I can be much more effective in helping him or her to overcome a problem or just find out more about him or herself and his or her karmic cycle. A number of so-called conincidences can be traced back to prior lives, and these scenes can be most helpful to the patient in helping to explain why certain things have happened to them.

Shielding or protective techniques are always applied to a patient undergoing a past life regression. In all of the thousands of regressions that I have done, I have never had a traumatic episode or any type of negative experience. I shield with what I call "spiritual protection." This technique consists of having the patient imagine a pure white light entering the top of the head and filling the entire body, surrounding each and every muscle, bone and organ. That is all there is to it. This white light is to protect the patient from any harm or negativity that he might experience.

The case of Andy will illustrate the benefits of this technique. Andy is a blue collar worker who joined a coven in Baltimore because of his wife's interest in witchcraft. He quickly lost interest in this coven because of the many negative things that they were doing. He and his wife stopped going to the meetings but he started having hallucinations. At his job he would hear voices of people who weren't there and see shadows of people which would disappear when he turned around. One day he received a call from the coven leader telling him that these hallucinations would not stop until he rejoined the coven.

Andy came to me for help. He proved to be an excellent hypnotic patient, and after three sessions of spiritual protection his problems ceased. All I did was to protect Andy from the psychic attack he was receiving from the coven leader and his followers. The white light is to ward off any negative influence, regardless of the source. After a time the coven leader realized Andy was protected and no longer attempted to harass him with this form of negativity. Andy was free. (Let me say at this time that I advise everyone to stay away from any form of witchcraft, black or white magic, and especially covens. They are all negative and your karma, as well as your present life, may be made unpleasant by these groups.)

PROGRESSION

Now that you understand the basics behind regression, let us discuss progression. Progression is going forward in time. It is used in any kind of regression to return the patient to the present. For example, let us assume you were regressed to the age of five. If I then wanted to move you forward to the age of eight, I would progress you three years on the count of five. Finally, I would progress you back to the present, just prior to concluding the session. This is called progression. You are never in danger of being trapped in the future.

Progression also has other uses. It can be used to see how a particular decision that a patient is considering will come out. For example, let us assume you are considering changing your job. You progress yourself two years in the future and you can find out if you did change jobs and whether or not it worked out to your advantage. Let me make clear that I am not referring to psychic experiences. I do not consider myself a medium or reader of the future. It is merely the use of hypnotic progression that enables me to help patients help themselves. I quite realize that there is no way to prove a progression other than waiting to see if a particular event occurs as seen in the progression.

Many people consider progression a form of wishful thinking. I will be the first to admit that the viewing of a scene in the future could possibly be the workings of hopes and desires of a subconscious mind, except for one fact. This fact is the viewing of scenes in the future of which the patient could have no control over establishing. An example of this would be reading a newspaper headline that exists five years in the future describing a natural disaster or the election of a President or a war, and having that event occur in five years just as it was read in trance five years before. No other explanation, in my opinion, could even come close.

SIMULTANEOUS TIME

In the last chapter, I briefly mentioned the lack-of-time concept. This concept offers us an interesting explanation as to the mechanism of a progression.

The lack-of-time concept states that the past, present, or future do not exist as isolated blocks of time. The past, present and future occur simultaneously and each can affect the other. Just because we are taught all through our academic years to think of the past as having occurred, the present as occurring and the future as about to occur, that is less than proof-positive of the way things are. Einstein's theory of relativity and quantum physics offer us far different possibilities of time.

If we assume for a moment that all time is occurring right now, then it is easy to see how one can read the future or past almost as easily as one reads the present. The placing of one's self in a hypnotic trance merely removes the usual barriers of time and allows for more complex observations.

The main problem in understanding the lack-of-time concept is that we function in a three-dimensional reality. There are many other dimensions that are illustrated by various forms of psychic phenomena. Time as we know it is merely an illusion created by our own physical senses. Our five senses perceive reality as occurring a little bit at a time. It thus appears that one event exists and is gone forever and is replaced by the next event which also disappears. Since our perception is limited, we nicely place time into three separate components called past, present and future.

An example of this concept is the dream state. Imagine having several dreams in a particular night. Each dream may encompass one hundred earth years but to you, the dreamer, only minutes have passed. During the dream state your subconscious mind is freed of the dimension in which time, as we know it, exists.

Since what we term past, present and future events appear to us in sequence, we find the idea of simultaneous time difficult to accept. Since, in that scheme, all events would occur at the same moment, a past event really doesn't cause a present one, nor does a present event cause a future one. Thus, our past and future lives really don't have to happen as we think they do. By changing our present circumstances we can effectively change our karma.

Think of how much karma could be removed by dealing with the past, present and future lives all at the same time. By the same token, think of how much karma can be added on instead of removed. This should actually give us more incentive to become a better person now.

Let me use the dream state again to illustrate the concept of no time. Some parapsychologists feel that when we dream we are being advised by our Masters and Guides on another dimensional plane. Since we are on a different plane, time has no meaning for us. We are shown how to work out our karma. We are taken to what we on the Earth plane would call the future.

Many people tell of having dreams of flying or of falling great distances. It has been postulated that this is a conscious remnant of the projection into the future that we experience in our dream state. The term *astral projection*, or *out of body experience* (OOBE), has also been used to describe this state. We all leave our body when we dream. The dream state for all of us is a communication between our dimension, or reality, and others'.

To understand the concept of creating your own reality, review the lack-of-time concept. If the present can directly change the past and future, you create your own reality every moment you exist. You alone are totally responsible for your life and the environment in which you live. Look within yourself for the causes of your good or bad fortune. Remember, karma is cause and effect.

DEJA VU VERSUS SYNCHRONICITY

When I give lectures on karma, I am often asked about the many coincidences that seem to occur in people's lives. As a parapsychologist I long ago dropped the term *coincidence* from my vocabulary. The term *synchronicity* is far more accurate.

Carl Jung, the Swiss psychiatrist, coined the word synchronicity. He used it to describe particularly meaningful occurrences without any apparent cause. This synchronicity seems to happen to people just at the right time and place. When you most require a certain chain of events to occur and they do, despite seemingly impossible odds, then you are experiencing synchronicity. ESP, telekinesis, psychokinesis, astrology, omens, *deja vu*, and precognitive dreams are examples of this principle.

The following is a possible physiological explanation of synchronicity: There are two hemispheres of the brain, the left and the right. Synchronicity actually entails the communication of the intuitive right brain (the subconscious and superconscious) with the analytical left brain (the conscious mind) through the use of symbolic events. Thus, these so-called coincidences represent the purposeful communication of the subconscious and superconscious minds with our conscious minds. Since the right hemisphere of our brain contains all knowledge of past, present, and future lives through the Akashic records, and since the left hemisphere of our brain barely keeps up with our present life, it is no wonder that consciously we call these events a "coincidence" and dismiss them from further thought or consideration. I personally feel that absolutely nothing happens by mere chance or coincidence.

Everyone has had experiences with *deja vu*. When you walk into a building that you know you have never seen or been in before but somehow feel that you have been there, you are experiencing what psychologists call *deja vu*. The classical explanation states that in this building you may see some furniture, paintings, curtains, or other structures with which you are familiar. The mind then simply extrapolates (extends beyond this association) the entire environment as being familiar.

In my opinion, this explanation just doesn't work. Many times patients have reported to me that absolutely nothing in the building seemed familiar—yet they knew they had been there before. It is my theory that one of two things has occurred. The most likely possibility is a progression. Perhaps a week before you visited this building, your subconscious mind read this event. Then, when the event became a reality, you felt strangely familiar with it. This sometimes happens to me in reference to conversations. I could be talking to someone and all of a sudden I know exactly what they are about to say next.

The second explanation, occurring less often, is the possibility that you had a past life in this building or a significant past life event occurred in or around the building. This has explained many of the spontaneous regressions that have been reported to me.

A good example is a young woman who came to me for a past life regression in 1978. She told me nothing about her background or experiences before I hypnotized her. Then, in the trance state, she described in detail a life in medieval Germany. She had travelled to Germany the previous summer on a vacation and was supposed to leave for Belgium, but was delayed unexpectedly for 24 hours. To kill time she went to a castle which had been converted into a museum. While in this castle she viewed a portrait of one of its residents, dating back to the thirteenth century. She spontaneously went into a regression and relived the life of this woman. She couldn't move a muscle during the experience, which lasted about 45 minutes.

Her purpose in coming to me was to confirm certain details about the regression, which she fortunately was able to do. Since this young woman was from Baltimore and had absolutely no interest or background in German history, I cannot accept the classical explanation of *deja vu* for this spontaneous regression.

DOCUMENTATION

Many people have asked me to use progression to predict the outcome of elections, stock market prices, etc. I will not do this for many obvious reasons, most important being the possible influence on the public as well as the creation of panic if a natural disaster is foreseen. Until this field is thoroughly investigated, I, myself, have more questions than answers.

When dealing with past life regression, the question of verification always comes up. Of course, many regressions have been thoroughly documented. A simple progression can be documented if you are patient enough to wait until the expected event is to happen. But how do you document a future life progression? The answer is simple—you don't. Waiting a few lifetimes or hundreds of years goes beyond even my patience. One day science may come up with an answer, but until that time this must remain an unsolved mystery.

In June of 1981 I conducted a rather unusual experiment. Charlie Donovan is the host of an evening talk show on WFBR radio in Baltimore. Since February of 1981 I have been the show's contributing editor on hypnotherapy and have many times discussed regression and progression on the air. Charlie called me on Friday, June 5th, to request my help in breaking the Baltimore Oriole's five-game losing streak. The Orioles were to play the

California Angels that weekend in Anaheim. Prior to that day the Orioles had lost three straight games to the New York Yankees. I progressed myself to the following day to see if I could visualize the box score of the game. The score I came up with was 6 to 3 in favor of the Orioles. During dinner that evening I thought of the score of 6 to 4 but dismissed it because the first impression is usually more accurate.

At 9:15 P.M. Eastern Standard Time I went on the air and had the listeners concentrate on the score "Baltimore 6 and California 3." I do not in any way consider myself to be a psychic, merely a hypnotherapist. For approximately one minute there was silence on WFBR as about 125,000 people concentrated on this score. At 9:25 P.M. I said goodbye to Charlie and my fans. The game began at 10:30 EST.

The score was 6 to 3 in favor of the Orioles by the middle of the seventh inning. A passed ball by the Baltimore catcher in the bottom of the seventh inning resulted in the final score being Baltimore 6 and California 4. The box score read as follows:

BALTIMORE   3 0 0   1 0 2   0 0 0   6

CALIFORNIA   0 0 1   0 0 2   1 0 0   4

Mass utilization of 125,000 subconscious minds seemed to have broken their losing streak.

There were 125,000 witnesses to this live demonstration of progression. I don't know exactly why or how this experiment worked, but there may someday be an answer.

CHAPTER SIX

DIDN'T WE MEET IN A PAST LIFE?

Love relationships are by far the most rewarding of all karmic entanglements. Couples quickly find out that they have been together before in many past lives. They will also be together again in future lives. When there is a problem in a relationship, past life regressions can often pinpoint the exact cause of the problem. One partner may have deserted his wife in a past life and thus incurred a karmic debt. In the life prior to that one the wife that was deserted may have deserted her husband or perhaps she accidently caused his death. Thus, a cycle of karmic debt and retribution was established.

This cycle will continue until all of the lessons are learned and all of the negativity is balanced by positivity. The principle of forgiveness will help speed up this process, but the cooperation of both members is necessary. Carl's case nicely illustrates these principles.

Carl came to see me several years ago. He was bothered by what is referred to as secondary impotency. This means that Carl is able to function sexually at some times, but not at other times. Physiologically there was nothing wrong with Carl, but psychologically he had problems. He was very much distressed when he came to my office. His voice was always soft and somewhat high pitched.

After working with Carl for six weeks I felt that the cause of his impotency was rather straightforward. A simple age regression revealed a scene in which Carl was in his present wife's (Martha) apartment. Martha was divorced at that time and she and Carl had been dating for about six months. On a fateful Sunday morning in June, Carl was in bed with Martha when his sleep was disturbed by a loud knock on Martha's front door. Carl was very groggy at the time so that he didn't consciously remember

this incident, although he readily re-explored it in trance.
Martha's ex-husband was at the door. He saw Carl's truck out
front and he was threatening Martha. He said that he knew that
Carl was in her bedroom and if he ever caught them making love
he would kill Carl. Carl's subconscious mind heard this and it
was the beginning of their sexual problems.

Carl was rather impressed with this regression because his impotency episodes almost completely disappeared within two
weeks. However, I was not satisfied that this was the true cause
of Carl's impotency and I suggested past life regression. Carl
was not sure about reincarnation, but he was willing to try anything that might solve his sexual problems.

Several weeks later Carl had his first past life regression. He
described a life in the 18th century in France. Carl was the son of
a fisherman in a small seaport on the east coast of France. His
name was Ladin. Gene was his best friend and Gene's father
owned most of the boats in this town. At the age of fourteen
Carl's (Ladin) father died and Carl became a fisherman working
with Gene. The following conversation represents Ladin at age
24:

Dr. G.:   Are you still working for Gene's father?
Carl: No.
Dr. G.:   What happened?
Carl: Gene, he's got all of the boats. His father died. Gene
          is my buddy. I got my own boat now.
Dr. G.:   Do you enjoy your work?
Carl: Yeah. Especially when she goes with me.
Dr. G.:   Who is she?
Carl: Jeanne, my girl Jeanne.
Dr. G.:   How long have you known Jeanne?
Carl: About two years.

Carl's voice had dropped to a very low level at this time. He
now spoke with great confidence.

Dr. G.:   I want you to move forward to a very important event
          that occurs between you and Jeanne on the count of
          five.   One . . . two . . . three . . . four . . . five.
          What do you see now?

Carl: We're sitting right there at the table. She is going to the doctor.

Dr. G.:   What is wrong with Jeanne?

Carl: She doesn't have long.

Dr. G.:   She doesn't have long to live?

Carl: No. That's not it. She's pregnant, but they're not sure whether the baby will make it.

Dr. G.:   Are you married to Jeanne now?

Carl: Yeah.

Dr. G.:   I want you to move forward to after the time Jeanne sees the doctor. One . . . two . . . three . . . four . . . five. What do you see now?

Carl: The doctor—he must be a quack.

Dr. G.:   Why?

Carl: He don't know nothin'. He don't know what to do. I have to stay with her all the time.

I progressed Carl to the day of the birth of his child.

Dr. G.:   What is happening now?

Carl: Jeanne, she is screaming.

Dr. G.:   Where is the doctor?

Carl: He's not there. There's some woman there instead.

Dr. G.:   What happens next?

Carl: It's all over. My baby is lost (crying).

Dr. G.:   All right, Ladin, detach yourself from any negative emotions and tell me exactly what happened.

Carl: They couldn't save him. I, I feel it's my fault. Oh, my God, Jeanne's dead! She died giving birth to a dead baby. It was a boy. I'll never go through that again.

Carl made up his mind not to have children again. His subconscious mind could very well have interpreted that literally by causing him to be impotent. After progressing Ladin ahead five years in time, the following information was obtained:

Dr. G.:   Where are you living now?

Carl: I'm living in town.

Dr. G.:   What are you doing?

Carl: I got a shop. I make fishing nets. I'm respectable.
Dr. G.:   How is business?
Carl: Pretty good. My pa, he should have done this.
Dr. G.:   What happened to Gene?
Carl: I, I don't see him.
Dr. G.:   Where does Gene get his nets from?
Carl: He sure doesn't get them from me.

Carl was progressed to his death. I then contacted his super-conscious mind and questioned him about his life as Ladin.

Dr. G.:   How does Gene relate to your life as Carl?
Carl: Gene is Randy.
Dr. G.:   Who is Randy?
Carl: My little brother.
Dr. G.:   Who is the entity known as Jeanne?
Carl: She's my wife, Martha.
Dr. G.:   Who was your father, the fisherman?
Carl: He is my Uncle Charlie.

From the superconscious mind level the patient can identify people from a past or future life and inform me who they are in their present life. Carl as Ladin blamed himself for Jeanne's (Martha's) death as well as that of their baby boy. By becoming impotent he eliminated the possibility of putting Martha through another traumatic pregancy.

The less experienced therapist might be satisfied with this regression as the cause of Carl's present impotency. However, there are usually a series of lives and incidents relating to any problem. One must go beyond this regression and continue to search for other causes. On December 29th Carl was regressed into another past life. He described a life in the 14th century in Germany.

Dr. G.:   What is your name?
Carl: Hans.
Dr. G.:   What is it that you do?
Carl: I take care of the castle.
Dr. G.:   Where do you live?
Carl: In a small room in the back of the castle.
Dr. G.:   Who owns the castle?

Carl: The lord. He lives there with his wife.
Dr. G.:   How old are you now?
Carl: Fifteen.

Carl was progressed to the age of 20.

Dr. G.:   What do you do for a living?
Carl: I'm a soldier.
Dr. G.:   Where do you fight?
Carl: I protect the castle.
Dr. G.:   From whom?
Carl: Beggars and invaders.
Dr. G.:   Move forward five years on the count of five. One . . .
          two . . . three . . . four . . . five. Are you still a
          soldier?
Carl: Yes. I command 300 men.
Dr. G.:   Do you have a woman?
Carl: Helena. Helena is the most beautiful woman in the
          world.
Dr. G.:   Are you married to Helena?
Carl: No. She is the daughter of the lord (the owner of the
          castle).
Dr. G.:   On the count of five I want you to move forward to a
          significant event, if any, that occurs between you and
          Helena. One . . . two . . . three . . . four . . . five.
          What do you see now?
Carl: I'm all dressed up. I've got my shields on.
Dr. G.:   What is the occasion?
Carl: I'm marrying Helena.
Dr. G.:   How do you feel?
Carl: I feel great (very excited).

Carl was then progressed forward to the birth of his first child.

Dr. G.:   What do you see now?
Carl: My baby.
Dr. G.:   Is it a boy or a girl?
Carl: It's a boy, a baby boy.
Dr. G.:   Where are you living now?
Carl: I have a small house near the castle.
Dr. G.:   Who lives in the castle now?

Carl: The lord's wife. The lord died and now his wife lives there.

Dr. G.:   Are you still a soldier?

Carl: Yes, and I'm damn good at it too.

Dr. G.:   How do you get along with the lord's wife?

Carl: I don't like her. I told her to get out of the castle. It's mine and I want it.

I progressed Carl forward to a scene which would show a resolution of this problem, if any existed. He was now 45 years old.

Dr. G.:   Where are you living now?

Carl: In the castle.

Dr. G.:   Where is the lord's wife?

Carl: I threw her out. She's crazy.

Dr. G.:   Why do you say that.

Carl: My soldiers forced her and her people out, but she makes trouble.

Dr. G.:   What kind of trouble?

Carl: She says things about me and she is trying to organize another army to attack my castle.

Carl was progressed forward to a scene which would signify a resolution to the problem with the lord's wife. He reported an attack on the castle.

Dr. G.:   What is happening now?

Carl: The soldiers are inside my castle and they're killing my men.

Dr. G.:   Do you recognize these soldiers?

Carl: Yes. They came once before with her (the lord's wife) about two years ago to try and get me to leave the castle. I wouldn't leave. It's my castle and I'm not leaving.

Dr. G.:   Where are your wife and child now?

Carl: Oh, dear God, they're dead! She (the lord's wife) did this. I'll get back at her if it's the last thing I do.

Carl died that day. He was killed by one of the soldiers and the lord's wife eventually moved back into the castle. When I spoke to Carl's superconscious mind, I found out that the lord's wife in that lifetime is his present wife (Martha). His statement concerning getting back at her was represented by his impotency. Carl was married before and never had any sexual problems until he met Martha. He was 35 years old when he met his present wife.

On January 19, 1979 I regressed Carl back into another life-time.

Dr. G.:	What do you see?
Carl:	Smoke. I see smoke.
Dr. G.:	Anything else?
Carl:	Tall trees. Many, many tall trees.
Dr. G.:	Are you in the woods?
Carl:	Yes. I'm outside my cabin. It's cold out and I'm gathering wood for the fireplace.
Dr. G.:	Can you see yourself?
Carl:	Yes.
Dr. G.:	What do you look like?
Carl:	I'm, I've got very long hair.
Dr. G.:	What color?
Carl:	Brown.
Dr. G.:	What is your name?
Carl:	Jake.
Dr. G.:	How old are you?
Carl:	Eleven.

Jake was born in 1802 in a cabin in Maine. His father's name was John and his mother was named Hilda. Jake did not go to school. He had a sister named Becky.

Dr. G.:	Can you read and write?
Carl:	Yes.
Dr. G.:	Who taught you?
Carl:	An old lady comes up from the village to learn me.
Dr. G.:	Do you like her?
Carl:	Yes, but sometimes she hits me on my fingers with a stick when I say something wrong.
Dr. G.:	What do you do with your time?
Carl:	I hunt. I like to hunt.
Dr. G.:	Who do you hunt with?
Carl:	I mostly hunt with Pa, but I like hunting with my buddy, Sam.
Dr. G.:	What do you hunt?

Carl: Deer, mostly.

Jake was progressed 10 years in time.

Dr. G.:   How old are you now?
Carl: Twenty-two.
Dr. G.:   Do you have a girlfriend?
Carl: Yeah.
Dr. G.:   What is her name?
Carl: Amy.
Dr. G.:   How did you meet her?
Carl: She works in the general store in the village. I met her
           there.
Dr. G.:   How do you get along?
Carl: She likes me a lot but she doesn't want me to hunt.

I progressed Jake ahead five years to the age of 27. His father
had died and he had left home to start his own life. He and Sam
bought a small farm and hunted together often.

Dr. G.:   Where are you now, Jake?
Carl: I'm in my room, thinking. [Jake's voice was very deep.]
Dr. G.:   What are you thinking about?
Carl: I killed a fox yesterday. I hate them foxes.
Dr. G.:   Where is Amy?
Carl: I don't got time to fool with no woman. She wouldn't
           come with me when I moved here.
Dr. G.:   Where is Sam?
Carl: He's out hunting deer.
Dr. G.:   Why aren't you hunting with him?
Carl: I didn't feel like it today. I just want to think awhile.
Dr. G.:   What are you thinking about?
Carl: Things.
Dr. G.:   What kind of things.
Carl: Last week I almost shot Sam. He got real mad at me.
Dr. G.:   Is that why you didn't go hunting with Sam today?
Carl: Yeah. Hey, why all these damn questions? Just who
           the hell are you anyway?

This sometimes occurs in trance. If a patient is re-living an
uncomfortable scene, he or she may become somewhat indignant

to my voice. They will demand to know who I am. Fortunately, this effect is temporary and questioning can resume in a few minutes.

Dr. G.:   How are you and Sam going to solve this problem the next time you go hunting?

Carl: We worked out some signals. When me or him whistle a certain way that means it's us and not some damn animal.

Jake was then progressed ahead to an important event that occurred between him and Sam.

Dr. G.:   Where are you now?

Carl: I'm in the woods.

Dr. G.:   What are you doing?

Carl: I'm hunting. What else would I be doing here?

Dr. G.:   Are you alone?

Carl: Nah, Sam is hunting with me. He's out somewhere ahead of me.

Dr. G.:   How does Sam feel about hunting with you again?

Carl: Oh, he's okay. We worked out a plan to get some deer. We haven't killed a deer in over two weeks.

Dr. G.:   Where exactly are you now?

Carl: Quiet.

Dr. G.:   What's happening.

Carl: Be quiet. Can't you hear that?

Dr. G.:   No. What is it? What do you hear?

Carl: There's something moving in the bushes. I'm gonna get me one of them deer.

Dr. G.:   Did you kill it?

Carl: I don't know. I shot it and the bushes stopped moving. I better see if I got it.

Dr. G.:   Did you kill the deer?

Carl: Oh, my God. I shot Sam. He's hurt real bad. Why the hell didn't he whistle?

Dr. G.:   What is happening now?

Carl: I'm trying to get him back to the house.

Dr. G.:   What is he saying to you?

Carl: Nothing. He's unconscious.

Dr. G.:   How far are you from the house?
Carl: Just a couple of miles.
Dr. G.:   Move forward to the time when you and Sam are back
          in the house at the count of three. One . . . two . . .
          three. What is happening now?
Carl: I'm going into the village to get the Doc. I sure wish
          I didn't have to leave Sam here alone.
Dr. G.:   Is he still unconscious?
Carl: Yeah. He don't look good.

I progressed Jake to the completion of this event. It seems that
he had a difficult time finding the doctor. A local bar was where
the elderly physician spent much of his time. Jake found him
there shooting pool and finally convinced him to come out to the
cabin. The doctor attended to Sam, but it was hopeless. It was
just a matter of time before Sam died.

Dr. G.:   What is going on at this time, Jake?
Carl: The Doc, he can't do much for Sam. Sam's gonna die.
          It's all my fault.
Dr. G.:   Is Sam conscious now?
Carl: He's lost a lot of blood. He can barely talk.
Dr. G.:   What is he saying?
Carl: He says that it all happened so fast. He didn't know
          where I was.
Dr. G.:   What does he say to you?
Carl: He says 'don't touch me.' He tells me I'm stupid and
          that he wished he never knew me. He looks so pale.
Dr. G.:   How do you feel, Jake?
Carl: I'm so ashamed. It's all my fault. I should have whistled
          before I shot into the bushes.

I removed Jake from this scene and progressed him forward.
It seemed that Jake's life went downhill after Sam died. He left
the farm and moved into the mountains. He built a small cabin
there and hunted and fished most of the time. It was a very lonely
life and Jake was most relieved when death finally came. I took
him to the superconscious mind level and asked him some final
questions:

Dr. G.:   How do you feel about your life as Jake?

Carl: I didn't do anything right. I was so lonely. If only I
           didn't shoot Sam.
Dr. G.:   Who was Hilda? Who is Hilda in your present life?
Carl: The secretary, Pam, down at work. That's who Hilda is.
Dr. G.:   What about John? Who is John?
Carl: Daniel. He's one of my buddies at the plant.
Dr. G.:   Who is Becky?
Carl: She's my sister-in-law.
Dr. G.:   What about Amy? Who is she?
Carl: Emily.
Dr. G.:   Who is Emily?
Carl: She was a girl that I dated when I was in high school.
Dr. G.:   Who was Sam?
Carl: Martha. Sam is Martha.

What is most important about this life is the death scene with
Sam. Sam said to Jake, "Don't touch me." He made Jake feel
guilty and useless. Carl's subconscious mind remembered this,
and his present impotency was a direct result of this incident.

This case illustrates the principle of changing sexes. Martha
was a male in her last life as Sam. Although most of your lives
will be lived as one sex, the karmic cycle requires at least one
change of sex.

When Carl was Ladin in the 18th century in France, he blamed
himself for Martha's (Jeanne's) death. She died in labor and Carl
promised himself that he wouldn't go through that experience
again. He didn't want to have any more children. In his next life
as Jake he would never marry. One might say that he indirectly
caused the death of Martha as Ladin, but as Jake he directly
caused Martha's (Sam's) death by accidentally shooting him. The
amount of guilt that Carl brought with him from these past lives
was enormous.

In the lifetime as Hans, Carl forced Martha (the lord's wife)
out of the castle. Martha won in the end and caused the death of
Carl. Carl swore that he would get back at her if it was the last
thing he ever did. He was good to his word as he sought karmic
retribution indirectly during his next two lives as Ladin and Jake.
His present life as Carl might have ended up the same way. Fortunately, Carl was able to see the causes of his sexual difficulties.

If I had regressed him further, I'm sure I would have found other lives in which Martha let him down and vice versa.

It doesn't matter who started the problem. All that really matters is that the problems get resolved. Today, Martha and Carl have no sexual problems. They love each other very much and have finally learned to live together in peace. It takes many lifetimes for most couples to finally resolve their difficulties.

CHAPTER 7

BOB AND THE "LIGHT PEOPLE"

There are many theories about the origin of our species. Anthropologists and paleontologists have strong opinions about Africa as the birthplace of man. Religious leaders have equally strong and conflicting theories. Parapsychologists have yet a very different explanation. Earlier in the book I spoke of the extraterrestrial concept of evolution and reincarnation. Although this is one of the most controversial aspects of parapsychology, Bob's case history might lend some credence to this theory.

Every so often I regress a patient only to find that they are not in a physical form. They do not possess a body. They are pure energy. The most common form of energy is light. The term "light people" has been used to describe entities that do not take physical form. Bob's case is actually quite typical of a "light people" regression.

In November of 1979 Bob called my office for an appointment. For the first time in his life he was suffering from insomnia. For the past two months, recurring nightmares had kept waking him in the middle of the night and he had found it difficult to fall asleep again. When he awoke the following morning he felt drained. It was obvious to him that he had experienced some traumatic dream during the night, but he did not remember the content. Also, his lack of energy was affecting his work.

Bob came to my office for his first appointment on a cold November afternoon. A medical technologist by profession, Bob was a highly intelligent and well-educated man in his late 30s. Parapsychology was not one of Bob's interests and he seemed somewhat anxious about being hypnotized. After hearing my explanations about hypnosis and asking some background questions, Bob settled down and was induced into a trance. At no time during this initial session did I discuss past life regression.

Most cases of insomnia can be treated easily enough without the use of regression. In routine cases I simply record a cassette tape that would relax the patient and program him to think of only pleasant thoughts before going to bed.

Bob was seen once a week for the next month and his insomnia disappeared. He was able to sleep soundly for the first time in three months. However, he did report an unusual dream to me, the only one he could remember. The environment of the dream was impossible to put into words. When he stated that all he could see around him were beams of light, I knew I had another "light people" regression in the making.

I explained the process of regression to Bob, being careful not to discuss past life regression of the "light people." The reason I handled this case in this way was two-fold. First, I didn't want to impose my belief system onto Bob. Second, I wanted him to enter a regression without any preconceived notions about extra-terrestrials.

Bob was quite willing to explore regression therapy. By this time he trusted me and held hypnosis in much higher esteem than he had the preceding month. After two sessions of simple age regression, Bob felt very comfortable with the technique. He was a good medium trance patient and a pleasure to work with. Highly intelligent people with excellent powers of concentration make the best hypnotic patients. Bob had both of these qualities in abundance.

On December 20, Bob was to be the recipient of a most unusual Christmas present. I always allocate additional time when I know in advance that this type of regression is going to be performed. The reason for this, as you will see shortly, is that there are many obstacles to a free flow of information. In most regressions, once a patient begins to answer questions, the information begins to flow rather freely. This is definitely not the case with a "light people" regression. After Bob was induced into a good medium trance, I asked him to go back to the origin of the nightmares that he had been experiencing. He reported a most unusual story.

Dr. G.:   What do you see at this time?
Bob: What is your vibrational rate?

Dr. G.:   Where are you now?

Bob: I, I can't see your essence. What is your vibrational rate?

Dr. G.:   It is your function to report your progress to me at this time. Your vibrational rate will be altered downward if you don't cooperate.

Bob: I have just been in the evaluation chamber. They won't tell me my exact progress.

Dr. G.:   Who are they?

Bob: Silence.

Dr. G.:   Who are they?

Bob: The Planners. Aren't you one of the Planners? No, I'm being directed not to tell you anything.

Before I continue with this regression I should explain that the "light people" are very restricted in what they can say. It is almost as if there is some sort of magnetic field around them that severely limits their ability to communicate. My vocabulary may seem different during this regression. The reason I am able to elicit any information whatsoever is due to the fact that I have performed a number of these "light people" regressions and I can relate to them on their level of awareness.

Dr. G.:   What is your name?

Bob: I, I have no name. I am merely a source with a vibrational rate.

Dr. G.:   What is your vibrational rate?

Bob: Silence.

Dr. G.:   What is your vibrational rate?

Bob: I am not permitted to release that information. They won't let me. I know that you're not a Planner. Why can't I see your essence?

Dr. G.:   I am not a Planner but I do monitor your progress. My vibrational rate is well beyond yours so that you cannot detect my essence. Now tell me about your experiences on the planet.

Bob: I don't want to go back. The physical form is not pleasant. I don't like it.

Dr. G.:   What do you see around you at this moment?

Bob: I am in a chamber of some sort. I have never been in this place before. My source is yellow. There are other sources of different colors present. We are in formation. The Planners are giving us orders.

Dr. G.:   Can you describe the room that you are in?

Bob: The chamber is white. There are no distinct borders. Everything is hazy. There is much movement of different sources. We are being judged.

Dr. G.:   Who is judging you?

Bob: The Planners. They are evaluating our trials with the physical form on the planet. I know I've done poorly.

Dr. G.:   Why do you say that?

Bob: It's awkward being in those things. Why do they want us to be physical? Can you help me?

Dr. G.:   You know I can't. I'm not permitted to interfere with the Planners. My purpose is strictly to gather information. What is happening now?

Bob: The Planners have not allowed us to leave our places. I can't move. One of the sources is being reduced for his actions on the planet.

Dr. G.:   What do you mean by reduced?

Bob: The vibrational rate is being lowered. It will mean more time in the physical form.

Dr. G.:   Where are you from?

Bob: We are not from this galaxy. I am not permitted to give you any more details about our planet.

Dr. G.:   Why did you come to this planet?

Bob: To explore. The Master Planners want us to experience the physical form. It is our mission. We are supposed to help those forms on the planet. I just want to go home but they won't let me.

Dr. G.:   Has any other source returned home?

Bob: No. We will stay here until the mission is complete.

My interpretation of further discussion with Bob is as follows: It seems that these "light people" were sent to the Earth to experience the human body. They were supposed to help our evolutionary progress. Many of these sources, or lights, failed in their initial attempts at taking over the body. Apparently, it was easy for them to come and go as they pleased. At regular intervals they were removed from the bodies and brought to some sort of examination room (although this was not a physical room as we know it). Their progress was evaluated by a group of monitors or Planners. If they did well, their vibrational rate was raised, but if they failed, it was reduced. These Planners were directed by Master Planners who communicated with them from the home planet many galaxies away.

Dr. G.: Why have you disturbed the entity known as Bob with these scenes during his rest period?

Bob: It was time he knew.

Dr. G.: Why now?

Bob: Before his vibrational rate was too low. It is now high enough for him to receive this data.

Dr. G.: Why not let him experience this data during his waking state?

Bob: I can't answer that. Only the Planners know that. I am not a Planner.

Dr. G.: How did you do on your last evaluation?

Bob: I failed some of the tests. I am going to have to spend more time in the physical form.

Dr. G.: Are you being disciplined?

Bob: Spending more time in the physical form is always a punishment. I must not fail again.

Dr. G.: What happens if you continue to fail?

Bob: I will not be able to leave the physical form. Can't you communicate with them and explain. . . . ?

Dr. G.: I cannot communicate with a Planner. What is it like in a physical form?

Bob: Silence.

Dr. G.: What is it like in a physical form?

Bob: They won't allow me to communicate. Only the Planners can know that. You must accept that.

Dr. G.: I understand.

Bob was progressed forward in time to the final outcome of his experiences as one of the "light people." He reported having failed many additional tests and was not permitted to leave the human body. During the latter stages of this regression, it became increasingly difficult to obtain any information. Bob was being censored. The words came out slowly and only with great difficulty. I brought him back to the present and gave him many suggestions for relaxation.

Dr. G.:   Well, Bob, how did it feel?

Bob: I, I don't know what to make of it. I felt as if I was in a bubble of some sort. My every thought was being controlled. It is by far the most unusual experience I can ever recall.

Dr. G.:   Did you know who I was?

Bob: Absolutely not. Your voice bothered me at first because I couldn't see your light. I don't know why that was particularly important, but it was.

Dr. G.:   Did you feel more comfortable after I identified myself?

Bob: Yes. I felt more relaxed for a while, but sometime later that feeling of being controlled came back and I couldn't answer your questions. What does it all mean?

I explained the "light people" to Bob and told him why I kept him in the dark about this concept. Although he was quite skeptical at first, he seemed to understand and was grateful for the progress he had made.

During the next six months Bob kept in contact with me. His insomnia did not recur and the nightmares stopped. Apparently, he was free of this situation.

The nightmares had been scenes of his former incarnation as one of the "light people." By reviewing these scenes in a hypnotic trance the information from his prior life as one of the "light people" was given to him. This eliminated the need for further nightmares. Bob, to this day, is still quite skeptical about "light people." He is merely happy that he no longer has a sleeping problem.

"Light people" regressions are infrequent, but they always seem to occur at a significant time in a person's life. The state described may or may not be the cause of a problem, but the information that is received is always helpful to the patient. It seems that when the student is ready, the "light people" will be there. Usually, these "light people" explore their first incarnation on Earth. Most patients who have these types of experiences show very little interest in extraterrestrial life. They usually seek my services for habit elimination or some other problem.

There are many interesting concepts that "light people" regressions illustrate. All communication was done by telepathy. Some of the silences were attempts of the hypnotized patient to communicate with me by telepathy. These sources of light functioned on a different dimensional plane. The term "room" has a different meaning to them. These beings were pure light energy. The only things that could confine them were magnetic fields and thought patterns controlled by the Planners. A Planner could immobilize one of the "light people" merely by directing certain thoughts at them.

I have my own theories as to the origin of the "light people." Obviously, they are entities from another planet. Since the information that I have received is fairly consistent, I have ruled out hallucinations or overactive imaginations. One can only guess as to why our planet was chosen by these "light people." Perhaps we are fortunate that our evolution was tampered with by these aliens. Our present technology might have been impossible without their aid. In addition, these aliens may have added to, if not caused, our present karmic cycle by interfering with our development.

I wonder about our future. Scientists today feel that evolution will eventually eliminate the need for a physical body. Are we then all going to end up as "light people"? If we do, I hope we learn from the mistakes of our predecessors.

CHAPTER 8

HUBERT MEETS ALIENS IN ANCIENT EGYPT

Hubert is a rather kindly, sixty-year-old southern gentleman from Virginia. He called me in August of 1978 to request a past life regression. It seemed that he had been in Baltimore visiting his sister and had looked up hypnotists in the Yellow Pages. When he saw my name he wrote it down but did not call me before he left town. Out of the twenty names listed under hypnotists he picked mine. Synchronicity was working again.

It was a very humid afternoon when he called me from Virginia and asked if I did past life regressions. Interestingly enough, I am the only hypnotherapist in Baltimore who does engage in past life regressions. Hubert told me that he would be back in Baltimore in October, and he set up an appointment. He wanted to see me every day for a week before he left for Virginia. This is a most unusual request, but I honored it, and I'm glad that I did.

Hubert had recently heard of the concept of hypnotic regression and was most eager to begin. One important note about Hubert's background was that he was alone in this life. His wife had died about ten years earlier and his sister in Baltimore was one of his last living relatives. As a retired salesman Hubert felt very lonely.

We discussed hypnosis and past life regression at length during this initial session. During his second session, a simple age regression was performed. I was not overly impressed with the results. During the third and fourth sessions, however, Hubert entered into deeper trance levels and revealed a past life in Egypt.

Dr. G.: What do you see now?
Hubert: I'm standing in front of the pyramid.
Dr. G.: Is there anything else that you can see at this time?
Hubert: I see the Sphinx in the distance.
Dr. G.: Which object do you feel closer to?

Hubert: The pyramid, definitely.

Dr. G.:   How many pyramids do you see?

Hubert: Just the one.

Dr. G.:   Can you describe the pyramid?

Hubert: It is only partly built.

Dr. G.:   Can you see yourself in this scene?

Hubert: Yes. I seem to be lifting a large stone.

Dr. G.:   Are you alone?

Hubert: No. I am one of many workers involved in moving this rather large block of stone.

Dr. G.:   Is there anyone directing you?

Hubert: No, not at this moment. We seem to know what we're doing.

Dr. G.:   How are you moving these stones?

Hubert: We're moving them the wrong way. We're lifting them by brute strength. It is not being done scientifically. We are trying to get them into position to place ropes around them.

Hubert appeared to be very much bothered by the fact that there was little efficiency in the movement of these stone blocks. He felt he knew a better way but realized that nobody would listen to a mere worker.

Dr. G.:   How much of the pyramid is complete?

Hubert: About one third, roughly.

Dr. G.:   Are you living with anyone at this time?

Hubert: Yes, I'm married to a beautiful but shy woman.

Dr. G.:   Can you describe her to me?

Hubert: She's dark skinned and almost my age (18 years old). Her hair is long and black. We love each other very much.

Dr. G.:   How tall is she?

Hubert: About 5' 4". She is about two inches shorter than me.

Dr. G.:   Do you have any children?

Hubert: No, it's just us two.

Dr. G.:   At the count of five I want you to move forward to a very important event in your life. One . . . two . . . three . . . four . . . five. What do you see now?

Hubert: I'm in our tent and I'm playing with our child. He is a great source of pleasure to us.

Dr. G.:   Where are you living now?
Hubert: We are not far from the river. Our tent is small.
Dr. G.:   What kind of work do you do now?
Hubert: I'm a stone worker for the Great Pyramid.
Dr. G.:   How old are you?
Hubert: Thirty-one.
Dr. G.:   What exactly does your position involve?
Hubert: I cut slots into the stones so that they will fit into the pyramid.
Dr. G.:   Do you like your job?
Hubert: I'm very skillful at my work, but they won't listen to my ideas about moving the stones.
Dr. G.:   Who are they?
Hubert: The directors.
Dr. G.:   Can you describe these directors?
Hubert: They are very tall, around 7 or 8 feet tall. They have large heads and long fingers.

These seem to be aliens directing the construction of the pyramids. When I asked Hubert how they moved about from place to place, he described no vehicle. It seems that they just appeared at various sites about the pyramid and directed crucial steps in its construction. They then disappeared.

Dr. G.:   How do the directors communicate with you?
Hubert: They don't talk at all. They seem to send out some sort of thought signal which compels me to obey them. I, I don't feel that I can resist them at all.
Dr. G.:   How much of the pyramid is built at this time?
Hubert: About two-thirds.
Dr. G.:   I want you to move forward by at least ten years on the count of five. One . . . two . . . three . . . four . . . five. Can you tell me what you see now?
Hubert: I'm much older. My shoulders are rounded and most of my hair is gone.
Dr. G.:   Are you still working on the pyramids?
Hubert: Yes, but not as much now. They (the directors) realized that I couldn't work as hard as I did when I was younger, but they need my experience.
Dr. G.:   Where are your children now?

Hubert: My daughter is home and my older son works with a different crew on the pyramid.

Dr. G.:   Where is your younger son?

Hubert: He is not with me. He left home and I feel lonely without him.

Dr. G.:   Let's go back to the directors. How do they help you build the pyramid?

Hubert: They provide us with instructions and special equipment.

Dr. G.:   What kind of equipment?

Hubert: They have special ropes. I've never seen rope like it before. It is very strong and doesn't seem to break. They also have a crane-like apparatus that runs on a battery of some sort.

Dr. G.:   How many directors are present at one time?

Hubert: Three.

Dr. G.:   How much of the pyramid is built now?

Hubert: It's almost complete. Thank God. I feel as if my very soul went into that pile of stone.

The Great Pyramid of Giza was built by the Pharaoh called Khufu. There were three pyramids constructed between 2600 B.C. and 2500 B.C. The largest and oldest is called Giza. The ancient Greeks referred to Khufu by the name Cheops. This pyramid is located in the desert along the Nile River, about ten miles south of Cairo in Egypt. The pyramid is about 481 feet high and its square base measures 755 feet on each side.

Inside the bottom of the pyramid are large rooms that were used as tombs for the royal family. These rooms contained gold, precious gems, beautifully carved furniture and other valuable objects. The Egyptians believed that a dead person could take earthly possessions to heaven with him.

It is rather hard to imagine that the ancient Egyptians (almost five thousand years ago) were able to build this monumental structure without the aid of modern cranes and engines that we use in building today. Historians believe that the Great Pyramid of Giza took about twenty years to build and that at least 100,000 men labored to complete it. Most of these men were slaves who worked endlessly, hauling the large stones and somehow putting them in place.

Engineers have stated that in order for such a structure to remain standing after almost five thousand years, great accuracy must have been used in the placing of the stone blocks. An error in placement of about ¼ of an inch could have caused the complete collapse of this great pyramid in just a few hundred years. The average error on each side, however, is less than a ten-thousandth of an inch in squareness and in level.

Hubert was progressed another five years.

Dr. G.: What important event, if any, has occurred?

Hubert: My daughter got married. She moved out of our tent and I feel so alone now. The pyramid is completed and I have nothing to do.

Dr. G.: What happened to your two sons?

Hubert: The younger one never came back and my older son died in an accident while working on the pyramid. He was crushed—oh dear Lord, it was pitiful—by a large stone.

Dr. G.: What do you look like now?

Hubert: I'm a broken down old man. I have no hair. My wife is dead. Two of my children have gone. My daughter moved away. I don't like being alone.

Dr. G.: What kind of food do you eat?

Hubert: It's some sort of grain with water. Garlic is also part of my diet. Sometimes I eat fish.

Dr. G.: What do you drink?

Hubert: Water. Just water.

The remainder of Hubert's life was uneventful. He described his existence as that of a welfare recipient. He received no money but food and clothes were given to him. He was moved into a small hut where he lived out the rest of his life by the Great Pyramid. The directors used him now and then to teach the younger stone workers. Hubert enjoyed the company of these young workers. This part-time occupation kept him from feeling totally useless and alone.

The last step in this regression was to take Hubert to the super-conscious mind level to find out how these people fit into his karmic cycle. We discovered that his wife in Egypt was his wife in this life. His daughter and younger son had no connection with him in this life. The older son, however, was a sales manager of his about twenty years ago.

It is interesting to note Hubert's loneliness both in Egypt and in his present life. In his Egyptian life his wife died just a few years before he did, yet he felt alone and lonely much of his life. Hubert had a great deal of love for his children, but they never returned his affection.

There are many parallels between Hubert's Egyptian life and his present life. Today he is a very soft-spoken and shy man who wants so much to contribute, but nobody seems to listen. As a salesman his suggestions were often rejected by his younger sales manager (his older Egyptian son reincarnated). In the regression, he was afraid to mention his ideas about moving the stones for fear of punishment. Throughout this life, Hubert exhibited fear of authority figures. Initially, he was even afraid to call me for an appointment.

If there is one karmic lesson that Hubert learned from this life it was patience. He is by far one of the most patient people I have ever known. Loneliness was another experience that Hubert was to explore in both lives. He seemed to accept his present situation without bitterness or regret.

A few months after his last session, I received a letter from Hubert, telling me that he had become involved in a local charity. His life seemed to take on more meaning. Younger people he worked with as a volunteer showed him a lot of respect, and Hubert now felt wanted. He gave much of the credit to me and my work, but it was Hubert who helped himself. All I did was to provide some guidance.

CHAPTER 9

THE BABY THAT WAS 200 YEARS OVERDUE

Evelyn is a registered nurse who works in a Baltimore County hospital. She had seen me on a local television talk show ("Hello Baltimore") and she wanted to be regressed into past lives. She had some personal questions she wanted answered, and she felt that past life regression was indicated.

I first interviewed Evelyn on August 12, 1980. She was a twenty-three-year-old somewhat overweight young woman with a very troubled past. It seems that she felt she was always disappointing her boyfriends. They couldn't seem to explain what the problem was, but her relationships rarely lasted more than a few weeks. Evelyn never married but she did have a baby girl a year and a half old. She had no philosophical problems about having the baby, it was simply something she felt she had to do. Evelyn wanted to know through past life regression why she felt so strongly about wanting to have her child.

The father of Evelyn's daughter was a salesman named Merle. He was never informed of the pregnancy and to this day does not know of his daughter. Merle was also disappointed with Evelyn and had broken up with her just three weeks after they started dating. For some unknown reason, this short relationship with Merle had become important to Evelyn. It wasn't just the fact that he was the father of the baby, according to Evelyn. There was more to it than that. She wanted to know what was behind this part of her life.

I regressed Evelyn back into her childhood. She reported some rather detailed scenes and I was very satisfied with this regression. She was given a past life regression conditioning tape and we set up an appointment for her past life regression.

Evelyn was very optimistic and cheerful when she arrived for her session. She had experienced a number of dreams that were

highly suggestive of past life scenes since I last saw her. The induction went quickly and Evelyn entered into a deep hypnotic
trance.

Dr. G.:   Can you tell me what you see before you?
Evelyn: It's dark.
Dr. G.:   Do you feel the presence of anyone else?
Evelyn: No. I just feel that I'm going to get hurt.
Dr. G.:   Why do you feel that you are in danger?
Evelyn: I don't know. I'm just scared.
Dr. G.:   Do you hear anything?
Evelyn: Um, noises.
Dr. G.:   What kind of noises?
Evelyn: Animals.
Dr. G.:   Do these noises bother you?
Evelyn: Yes.
Dr. G.:   I want you to carry this scene to completion. Tell me
          what happens to you.
Evelyn: I don't like the animals. I can't see them. I'm running,
          running through the woods to my house. I can't think
          of anything other than getting home. I shouldn't have
          stayed in the woods so long. These berries that I came
          here to pick don't taste that good anyway. Wait a
          minute—I see my house. There it is. Oh, thank God,
          I'm home.

Evelyn was progressed forward to the following day. She lived
in a small village in Switzerland in the early 1800's.

Dr. G.:   How old are you?
Evelyn: Fourteen.
Dr. G.:   What is your name?
Evelyn: Lilly.
Dr. G.:   What does your father do?
Evelyn: He works with his hands. He is a carpenter.
Dr. G.:   Can you describe your house?
Evelyn: It's not a big house. It's nice.
Dr. G.:   Can you give me more details about the house?
Evelyn: It's simple. There's not many partitions but you know
          it separates into different rooms.

Dr. G.:   Do you have any brothers or sisters?
Evelyn: I don't have any sisters, but I do have a younger
           brother.
Dr. G.:   What is his name?
Evelyn: Derek.
Dr. G.:   What do you like to do most of all?
Evelyn: I like walking.
Dr. G.:   Do you have any friends?
Evelyn: I don't. I feel very alone. I don't know why.

Lilly was progressed five years into the future.

Dr. G.:   Can you tell me what you see now?
Evelyn: I'm sweeping.
Dr. G.:   Where are you sweeping?
Evelyn: It's my house. It's time for me to sweep up so I'm
           sweeping.
Dr. G.:   Can you see yourself?
Evelyn: Yes.
Dr. G.:   How old are you?
Evelyn: Nineteen.
Dr. G.:   Tell me what you look like?
Evelyn: I'm five feet four inches tall and very slim. My waist
           is so small (patient was giggling).
Dr. G.:   Who do you live with?
Evelyn: Will.
Dr. G.:   Who's Will?
Evelyn: He's my husband.
Dr. G.:   Can you describe him?
Evelyn: He's tall. He has deep blue eyes.
Dr. G.:   How long have you known Will?
Evelyn: A couple of years. I feel very comfortable around him.
Dr. G.:   What are you most looking forward to at this time?
Evelyn: Having a child.
Dr. G.:   Are you pregnant now?
Evelyn: No. Will and I have been talking about having a baby
           but we haven't had one yet.

Lilly was progressed to a very significant event that occurred
between her and Will.

Dr. G.:   Can you tell me what you see?
Evelyn: I'm crying.
Dr. G.:   Why?
Evelyn: Because I'm a failure.
Dr. G.:   Why are you a failure?
Evelyn: I can't have children.
Dr. G.:   Who told you that?
Evelyn: My father and Will.
Dr. G.:   How does Will feel about your not being able to have children?
Evelyn: He tries to hide it but I see his disgust.
Dr. G.:   How about your father?
Evelyn: He wasn't supportive at all.
Dr. G.:   What about your mother?
Evelyn: She's there.
Dr. G.:   What is her attitude?
Evelyn: She's very meek. She means well but doesn't know what to say.

Lilly described a very frustrating life. As she grew older she became more and more sensitive to the fact that she couldn't have children. All of her friends raised families. Lilly's parents didn't know how to relate to her. Will seemed to tolerate her, but there was no love between them. She tried everything to please him, but nothing worked. Will wanted children. He would not divorce her nor would he have affairs, but he was very disappointed in his wife's inability to bear him children.

I progressed Lilly to the last day of her life.

Dr. G.:   Did you ever have any children?
Evelyn: No.
Dr. G.:   Who is around you at this time?
Evelyn: Will's there.
Dr. G.:   Is there anyone else present?
Evelyn: No.
Dr. G.:   How old are you?
Evelyn: Fifty-four.

Lilly was progressed beyond her death to the "other side."

Dr. G.:   What sensations do you feel at this time?
Evelyn: I feel light.
Dr. G.:   What else do you feel?
Evelyn: Cold.
Dr. G.:   What do you see?
Evelyn: Colors. Many colors.
Dr. G.:   Do you see any people?
Evelyn: I see Will.
Dr. G.:   Is he still alive?
Evelyn: Yeah.
Dr. G.:   What is he doing?
Evelyn: He's pacing.
Dr. G.:   In this life as Lilly, what is it that you feel you didn't accomplish?
Evelyn: I couldn't give what I wanted to give.
Dr. G.:   Which was what?
Evelyn: A child, a child to Will. It meant so much to him.
Dr. G.:   What is it that you feel you did accomplish?
Evelyn: I was a good worker. I know that I was a good worker.
Dr. G.:   Did other people respect you for your work?
Evelyn: Yes, yes. Will was even proud of my work.

Lilly was taken up to the superconscious mind and asked some additional questions.

Dr. G.:   Who was Will in your life as Lilly? Is Will anyone you knew or now know as Evelyn?
Evelyn: Merle. Will is Merle.

This case illustrates some rather interesting principles of karma. First, Evelyn disappointed Will by not being able to have children. This was one aspect of their life together that brought about the most hardship. The karmic debt was then established. Failure to have children, coupled with Will's disappointment in her, left Evelyn with a rather severe karmic debt. Evelyn's subconscious mind felt that she was branded with a disappointing tendency. She felt that no matter what she did she would somehow disappoint any man that she was involved with.

This fear carried over to her present life. Every relationship she entered resulted in disappointment. It wasn't so much that she just met the wrong kind of man, although that was a factor, it was the way in which she projected herself—as a person who would disappoint you.

Evelyn is attractive, despite the fact that she is overweight. She tended to overcompensate for her self-image by acting seductive. She discussed with me how she would set out to seduce men, although in the back of her mind she knew that she was going to disappoint them. She continually tried to prove to herself that there was someone out there who would appreciate her. Clearly, she was going about this pursuit in the wrong way.

When Evelyn became pregnant, something changed. She was no longer the sterile Lilly. She was now fulfilling a nearly two-hundred-year-old wish, a wish to have a child. This was one of the most important episodes in her present life. It is interesting to note that she never even considered abortion. The karmic lesson was well learned. The fact that she was single made absolutely no difference. At least now she didn't disappoint herself. She proved to herself that she could, in fact, have a child.

The fact that Will (in Evelyn's life as Lilly) is Merle (in her present incarnation) is not as significant as it might be to Evelyn. Evelyn may have disappointed Merle in this life during their three-week affair, but a child resulted from this relationship. In their past life they were married for more than thirty-five years and no children resulted from the union. The karmic debt of fertility was paid. Merle simply had to father Evelyn's child. My only regret was that I was not able to work more with Evelyn on additional lives. I'm sure we would have traced back the origin of this karmic debt.

One last observation to make about Evelyn was her current weight problem. In her life as Lilly she was very slim and attractive. This present weight problem was probably caused by built-up frustrations during her life as Lilly. Lilly was a very hard worker, and that one quality pleased Will. Keeping herself slender and attractive and hard working were, in Lilly's mind, the only ways she could hold on to Will.

Shortly after her pregnancy, Evelyn started to lose weight. Today, one year later, she is much thinner than she was when I originally saw her, yet I didn't work with her on weight control. I didn't have to. The pregnancy and the knowledge of her past life as Lilly was more than enough. She no longer needs to punish herself or feel frustrated. She has also reported to me that her relationships with men have changed. She now feels self-confident, no longer assuming that she will disappoint men.

Lilly has finally satisfied Will's two-hundred-year-old wish. And Evelyn is well on her way to achieving happiness.

CHAPTER 10

HYSTERICAL BLINDNESS AND A PAST LIFE IN THE LONDON SLUMS

Many people ask me what hypnosis can really do. If, according to recent statistics, modern medical technology is only about 75 percent successful, can hypnosis make up that additional 25 percent?

There are many syndromes that modern medicine can't cure. Drugs can treat many symptoms temporarily, but such diseases as ulcers, colitis, anxiety, and depression are not caused by bacteria, viruses, or fungi. They can't be cured with medication alone. They are psychosomatic in their origin, and the subconscious mind has a great deal to do with the elimination of these disturbances.

But even more obviously in the realm of treatment through hypnosis is a category of illness referred to as "hysterical disorders." Included in this category are hysterical paralysis, hysterical deafness, and hysterical blindness. These disorders have absolutely no medical or organic cause. A complete physical examination by a specialist would reveal no medical reason for the patient's infirmity, yet the fact remains that the patient is unable to function in one of these areas.

The case that I am about to describe illustrates this principle with respect to sight loss. An attractive 25-year-old interior decorator was brought to my office early in January, 1978 by her boyfriend. Her name was Judy, and Angelo was her male companion. Angelo had called me earlier that day to make this emergency appointment. It seemed that the week before Judy had lost her sight without any warning and with no apparent cause.

Judy had never had problems with her eyes before and, in fact, didn't even wear glasses. She had been to an ophthalmologist

affiliated with Johns Hopkins University and all of the tests turned
out negative. In other words, there was no medical reason for
Judy to be unable to see. I had personally spoken with her
ophthalmologist and he verified these facts.

It wasn't easy to take a history from Judy since she was very
upset and depressed. However, I finally found out that Judy lost
her sight shortly after discovering Angelo taking amphetamine
pills. She had been dating him for over a year but he had not
informed her of his pill ingestion habit. Within five minutes
after inadvertently seeing Angelo take these pills, Judy had
screamed and lost her sight.

I asked her if she screamed because of some pain. She said that
she just had an uncontrollable urge to scream but did not feel
any form of pain. Judy was naturally anxious about whether or
not I could help her. I explained to her and Angelo what I knew
about hysterical blindness. I made no promises or guarantees,
but told her I would do my best.

Inducing a hypnotic trance requires only that the patient hear
the hypnotherapist, and since Judy's hearing was unimpaired,
this presented no problem.

Judy entered into a good medium trance rather quickly, which
surprised me, considering her depression and recent traumatic
experience. I conditioned her for a simple age regression to be
performed on her next visit. She left my office feeling relieved
and more relaxed.

The second session consisted of a simple age regression. I
instructed Judy's subconscious to search through its memory
banks and relive a scene or scenes that were directly responsible
for her current sight problems. She reviewed a number of childhood scenes, but nothing directly related to her present loss of
sight.

During the next week I saw Judy two more times and performed a number of simple age regressions. Again nothing of
significance surfaced. Past life regression was the only avenue we
hadn't explored, so we decided to try it.

Judy was very willing, but Angelo didn't share her enthusiasm.
I told them to discuss it and call me when they had made their
decision. The next day Angelo called to schedule a past life
regression. Judy told me she considered it her only real hope. If

the ophthalmologist at Johns Hopkins couldn't find a medical cause, then the origin of her blindness must be psychological. Since she had been sightless for nearly three weeks, she was desperate. Angelo didn't think much of hypnosis, but he was willing to try anything to help Judy.

I induced Judy into a medium level hypnotic trance and gave her subconscious mind the suggestion to return to the true origin of her present sight problems. For about five minutes she sat motionless in my recliner with her eyes closed. I could tell she was reviewing many scenes since her eyeballs were moving back and forth rapidly. (These rapid eye movements, or REMs, also indicate that a person is dreaming.)

Judy finally began to answer my questions in a high-pitched, childlike voice.

Dr. G.:	Can you tell me what you see now?
Judy:	Everything I like. (giggling)
Dr. G.:	Where are you?
Judy:	I'm with my daddy.
Dr. G.:	And where are you both right now?
Judy:	Daddy said I can have some candy. He said I can have three pieces. The shop is full of candy and stuff.
Dr. G.:	What kind of stuff?
Judy:	Oh, you know. Food and stuff.
Dr. G.:	How long have you been in the shop?
Judy:	We just got here. I can't make up my mind what to get. (giggling)
Dr. G.:	What is your name?
Judy:	Elsie. Do you want some candy too? (giggling)
Dr. G.:	No, thank you Elsie. Where do you live?
Judy:	In London, of course. Aren't you silly?
Dr. G.:	What is your father's name?
Judy:	Daddy.
Dr. G.:	I mean what do other people call your daddy?
Judy:	Mac.
Dr. G.:	Where is your mother?
Judy:	She went away. (Her voice became soft.)
Dr. G.:	Where did she go?
Judy:	I don't know. (Patient began crying.)

Dr. G.:   All right Elsie, calm down. On the count of five all
          negative feelings about your mother not being here
          will disappear and you will feel happy again. One . . .
          two . . . three . . . four . . . five. What kind of work
          does your father do?
Judy: He works in a place with machines, big machines.
          (Patient began giggling again.)
Dr. G.:   How old are you Elsie?
Judy: I'm six years old. (She sounded very proud.)

Elsie responded well to my questions. She quickly changed
her emotional responses from that of crying to giggling when I
gave her the appropriate instructions. Further questioning revealed the following past life.

Elsie lived in a very run-down apartment on the south side of
London in 1887. Her father was a factory worker in a textile mill.
Elsie's mother left her and Mac when Elsie was just three years
old because of Mac's drinking. This was not a pleasant life for
Elsie as she had no playmates and her father worked long hours.
Even when he did have time for her, he was usually drunk.

It was surprising how much Elsie loved Mac, since he beat her
often and spent very little time with her. The only real pleasure
he provided was an occasional trip to the candy shop at the
market. It was Elsie's short memory that allowed her to forget
about Mac's faults and deal only with a present pleasurable
experience.

I next progressed Elsie forward in time, asking her to remember the true cause, if any, of her present sight problem.

Dr. G.:   Where are you now, Elsie?
Judy: I'm outside playing. (She sounded very sad.)
Dr. G.:   Is anything wrong?
Judy: No.
Dr. G.:   Come on now, Elsie, you can tell me. What is bother-
          ing you?
Judy: Well, I don't have anyone to play with and everybody
          is in church.
Dr. G.:   Why aren't you in church?
Judy: Daddy doesn't believe in going to church. He says it's
          a waste of time.

Dr. G.:   Is this Sunday?

Judy: Yes. Can you play with me? (Patient began giggling again.)

Dr. G.:   I can't play with you, Elsie, but I would like to know some things about your daddy. Would you mind telling me more about him?

Judy: Oh, okay. (Patient sounded bored.)

Dr. G.:   Where is he now?

Judy: He's in the house, probably in his room. He always spends Sundays in his room.

Dr. G.:   How old are you now Elsie?

Judy: Eleven.

Dr. G.:   Does your daddy ever take you to the park or to the city on Sunday?

Judy: No, I can't remember the last time he took me anywhere.

Dr. G.:   Do you love your daddy?

Judy: Well, I, of course I do. (She hesitated a few seconds before answering this question.)

I next progressed Elsie forward, asking for the actual event that would explain her present sight problem. She had gone back into the apartment on this Sunday afternoon looking for her father.

Dr. G.:   Where are you now, Elsie?

Judy: I'm on the couch playing with my doll.

Dr. G.:   Where is your daddy?

Judy: He's in his room, I think.

Dr. G.:   What are you going to do now?

Judy: I'm going to sneak up on my daddy and scare him.

Elsie went to her father's room and quietly opened the door.

Dr. G.:   Can you see your daddy, Elsie?

Judy: Oh God, what is my daddy doing? Daddy, Daddy, please don't do that! (Judy had a look of absolute horror on her face.)

Dr. G.:   What is your daddy doing?

Judy: He, he's sticking himself in the arm and he has a rubber band on his arm. (Patient sounded very excited.)

Dr. G.:   What is he doing now?
Judy: Daddy, Daddy, don't hurt me! No, no I didn't mean
          to scare you. (Patient now was very upset.)
Dr. G.:   What is your daddy doing to you, Elsie?
Judy: He beat me, beat me bad. I hurt all over. (Patient was
          wincing.)

Mac had severely beaten Elsie for walking in on him while he
was in the process of injecting morphine into his arm. Elsie had
never seen her father inject himself before. Apparently alcoholism
wasn't Mac's only problem.

After he had beaten Elsie, Mac locked her in his closet for the
rest of that day. Elsie was in a state of shock. She hadn't eaten
all day and hurt from the beating. It wasn't until early the next
morning that she was released from the closet.

It was necessary to give Judy (Elsie) many calming suggestions
before bringing her out of the trance.

Dr. G.:   Judy, on the count of five, you will be back in the
          present, January, 1978, and you will remember every-
          thing that you experienced and re-experienced.
          One . . . two . . . three . . . four . . . five, awaken.
Judy: Wow, that was quite something! Dr. Goldberg, Dr.
          Goldberg, I can see you! You're very hazy but I can
          see you. (Patient was elated.)
Dr. G.:   Focus on my voice, Judy. When I snap my fingers, you
          will be able to see me clearly.

It took Judy about three minutes until she was able to see me
clearly. We went into my reception room to join Angelo and
explain to him what had happened.

When Judy saw Angelo take the amphetamine pill (an addictive drug) she associated this incident with watching Mac inject
morphine (also an addictive drug). Judy was severely beaten by
Mac for viewing something she wasn't supposed to see. Since
Angelo hadn't told her about his taking amphetamines, when
Judy accidentally happened in on him, her subconscious made
the association of seeing something she wasn't supposed to see.
Through the hypnotic regression, the cause of the blindness was
removed and the symptom (blindness) disappeared.

This experience brought Judy and Angelo much closer together. They had not been getting along well of late, even before this hysterical blindness incident occurred. As a result of this regression, their feelings for each other grew stronger.

In addition to restoring Judy's sight, this past life regression had other unexpected benefits for her. For one thing, she reported that her claustrophobia had disappeared. It seemed that being locked in the closet caused Elsie, and later Judy, to become afraid of confined spaces. By reliving this past life, the true cause of Judy's claustrophobia was elicited and removed.

Another interesting fact was brought to my attention. Judy told me that she had quit her last job with a well known interior decorating firm because she hadn't liked her boss. She hardly knew him and rarely saw him, but the few times she did see him he was either drinking or smoking. One day he had come into the office drunk from a lunch date and she had simply quit. It worried her that she couldn't explain why at the time, but he had made her feel so uncomfortable that she had had to leave. Clearly, Judy's former boss reminded her of Mac. The association that her subconscious mind made with his drinking compelled her to quit. Judy now understood what had motivated her behavior and was comfortable with her decision.

This was a most interesting and rewarding case. The fact that the cause of Judy's blindness was psychological made hypnotic regression the treatment of choice.

CHAPTER ELEVEN

ODONTIATROPHOBIA
AND THE BLACKSMITH

I receive many calls from patients terrified of having dental work performed on them. Negative conditioning is generally at fault. If a patient has a traumatic experience with a dentist as a child, a lasting negative impression is often left in the subconscious mind. This negative association of dentistry and a traumatic experience may affect the patient's attitude toward oral health care for the rest of his or her life.

When I received a telephone call from Miriam in September of 1978 I listened very carefully to her story. It seemed this 51-year-old housewife had a tremendous fear of dentists. She hadn't been to a dentist in over ten years and she knew that she had many dental problems. What is especially interesting about Miriam's case is that her dental fear was related to other problems in her life. She had a low opinion of herself and felt that if she could somehow eliminate this phobia, her relationships with her husband, children, and friends would also improve. In fact, she felt her entire life would benefit from ridding herself of this fear. The technical term for a fear of dentists is *odontiatrophobia*.

When Miriam came to my hypnosis office for her first appointment, I discussed her dental history. It seemed that she could not remember a single traumatic incident involving herself and dentistry. Her interests in working with hypnosis weren't just to feel comfortable in my dental office, they were more oriented to finding out why she developed the dental phobia in the first place.

Miriam was an excellent hypnotic patient and I decided to use simple age regression to find out if there were some traumatic childhood incidents involving dentistry that were being repressed by her conscious mind. After three sessions of simple age regression, I found nothing to indicate a cause for her odontiatrophobia.

My next step was to explain the possibility of a past life cause to Miriam. She seemed quite interested in my explanation of karma and reincarnation and although she was somewhat skeptical, she seemed to trust me and was willing to try almost anything to get to the cause of her phobia. I gave her a past life regression conditioning tape and we made an appointment a few weeks hence.

Miriam seemed excited when she entered my office on that fall afternoon. As usual, she went into a deep trance quickly and was quite relaxed.

Dr. G.: Can you tell me what you see at this moment?
Miriam: I'm, I'm standing in the middle of the street holding my right cheek.
Dr. G.: Why are you holding your right cheek?
Miriam: It hurts. My damn tooth hurts.

Miriam is a very soft spoken woman and in the four weeks that I had known her prior to this regression, she had never used any form of foul language. Now her voice dropped in pitch and her language became coarse. During most of this session she held her right cheek as if she was in severe pain, although consciously no such discomfort existed.

Dr. G.: What are you going to do about your tooth?
Miriam: Well, first I'm gonna go to that there saloon (she pointed straight ahead with her left hand) and commence to drown this damn pain with some whiskey.
Dr. G.: And then?
Miriam: And then I suppose I'll just have to have that damn tooth yanked.
Dr. G.: Who will remove the tooth?
Miriam: Oh, Smitty, of course.

Miriam reported that she lived in a small town in Kansas in 1838. There were no dentists in her area so she had to go to the local blacksmith, Smitty, for an extraction. There was a physician

in town but he did not perform any dentistry. It was not uncommon for blacksmiths and barbers to do dentistry at that time.

Dr. G.:   What is your name?
Miriam: Anna.
Dr. G.:   Anna, has Smitty ever taken out teeth from you before?
Miriam: Oh, sure he has. (Her voice sounded somewhat shaky
               now.)
Dr. G.:   You don't sound very happy about the idea.
Miriam: I'm not. Damn it. Damn this tooth. Damn Smitty.
               (Anna's voice was loud and angry.)

I progressed Anna forward a few hours. She had gone into the
saloon and drunk many glasses of whiskey to premedicate herself.
We discovered that her husband had died a few years earlier, and
she ran their small farm with just two hired hands. Anna was a
very strong and resourceful woman in this life and had many
friends. The only real problem area of her life was her teeth. She
never took proper care of them and had many dental problems.
Smitty had removed seven or eight teeth from her over the years,
and every time he extracted one, Anna went through pure hell.

Dr. G.:   Anna, on the count of five, I want you to move for-
               ward to the time Smitty will be removing your tooth.
               One . . . two . . . three . . . four . . . five. Can you
               tell me what you see now?
Miriam: Damn Smitty. His shop smells like horseshit. (Miriam
               had put her fingers up to her nose.)
Dr. G.:   Where exactly are you now, Anna?
Miriam: I'm in the back of Smitty's blacksmith shop. It is right
               next to his horse stalls and it sure stinks something
               bad here.
Dr. G.:   Where is Smitty?
Miriam: He is getting his apprentice, Paul, to help him.
Dr. G.:   What is happening now?
Miriam: Paul went to get one of Smitty's pliers and now they're
               both back. I'm sitting on this old wooden chair and
               Paul is holding my head back.

Since there was no anesthesia at this time, all forms of dentistry, which mostly consisted of extractions, were performed by
physically restraining the patient.

Dr. G.:   What is happening now?

Miriam: Smitty is standing over me now with the pliers in his hand. (Her voice was very shaky again.)

Dr. G.:   Where is Paul?

Miriam: He is behind me holding my head back.

Dr. G.:   Continue on, Anna.

Miriam: Smitty puts those damn pliers in my mouth. I can taste the rust on them. (She grimaces and holds on very tightly to the arms of my recliner.)

Dr. G.:   What happens next?

Miriam: He puts the pliers on my back tooth. It hurts so bad now. The whiskey isn't working.

Dr. G.:   Go on, Anna.

Miriam: He yanks real hard and I try to turn my head but I can't. That Paul is so strong. (Her knuckles were beginning to turn white because she was holding onto my chair so tightly.) My tooth. Yeoow. Yeoow. Yeoow.

Anna screamed so loud it gave me a start. In a moment she calmed down and sank back in the chair, exhausted. I let her rest for about five minutes and then resumed the questioning.

Dr. G.:   Anna, are you alright?

Miriam: Oh, yes, I'm fine now. That Smitty is o.k. He got that damned tooth with one yank. (She was very relieved now.)

Dr. G.:   Does your jaw hurt?

Miriam: No, not now. I'll be o.k. I'm bleeding but I know it won't be long before that stops.

Dr. G.:   What are you going to do now?

Miriam: I'm going to stop back at the saloon and get me some more whiskey. Then I guess I'll go home and try to forget about today.

I progressed Anna throughout this day and the next day. Surprisingly, she didn't develop an infection from the dirty pliers. Her resistance to disease was good. Anna was able to work on her farm the following day. She was quite a remarkable woman.

One of the interesting things I observed about this regression was that Miriam seemed to admire Anna. Anna's strength, assertiveness, frankness, and honesty were attractive qualities.

After this session was over, I discussed my observations with Miriam. Miriam agreed that she found Anna a most unusual and admirable woman. Anna's self-confidence and ability to get along with people represented quite a contrast to Miriam.

Miriam was skeptical about whether she had actually lived before as Anna, but we decided that she would return to me for much-needed dental work. During her treatment I filled a number of teeth, performed two root canals and crowned five additional teeth. Miriam showed very little apprehension and, throughout the entire treatment, was an excellent patient. What was even more interesting to observe was the other improvements in her life. Miriam was quickly becoming more self-confident and assertive. She reported to me a closer relationship with her husband and her children. Her friends and relatives also noted this behavioral change. Some asked her if she were taking some medication. Others asked her if she were seeing a psychiatrist. Miriam reported feeling like a different woman.

I may take credit for her dental improvement, but it was a combination of Miriam's understanding and her past life regression therapy that resulted in her other changes.

This case is one of my favorites not just because it illustrates removing a dental phobia, but because it illustrates the tremendous personality improvements that a patient is able to make once they are presented with the true cause of their problem. Whether it is in this lifetime or another, reliving and letting go of repressed emotions and negative scenes will, more times than not, result in great changes in the patient's life. I am happy to say that Miriam is still a dental patient of mine and is doing just fine in all aspects of her life.

CHAPTER TWELVE

THE 800-YEAR-OLD SYNCHRONICITY

When I appear on radio or television or am interviewed by a newspaper reporter, I am often asked to relate my most interesting case. Although I find all of them gratifying, one especially stands out in my memory, and it involves my favorite principle, *synchronicity*.

It is not uncommon for the same people to occur in several of a patient's past lives. Group karma works just that way—a husband and wife in one life may come back as a mother and daughter or a brother and sister in another lifetime. An acquaintance in one life will often appear again in future lifetimes. This phenomenon is well accepted. What is unusual about this particular case is the manner in which I investigated it.

Nearly five years ago, I received a call from a man who identified himself as Arnold. Arnold worked as an appliance salesman in a Baltimore department store and was calling me for hypnotherapy at his wife's suggestion. In further conversation it came out that Arnold was a very insecure man, and this was negatively affecting his ability as a salesman.

Arnold proved to be an excellent hypnotic patient. After six lessions, he began feeling better about himself. During these sessions I gave Arnold many suggestions to improve his self image and assertiveness. The tape I recorded for him contained these suggestions and helped him to believe more in himself. Regression was not used at this time because I like to stabilize the emotional level first. Once a solid emotional foundation is established regression therapy is more efficiently carried out. Arnold expressed no interest in exploring regression at this time. His self-confidence improved and his sales record very much reflected this progress. He seemed troubled about something else; however, he was unwilling at this time to discuss it with me.

It is not my policy or purpose to pry, so I did not force the issue. I simply told Arnold that it was obvious something else was troubling him, and if he didn't feel comfortable discussing it with me, there was nothing else I could do for him. I instructed him to continue playing the cassette tape I recorded for him. This case was far from complete, but since the patient closed all avenues of communication, I had no choice. Arnold thanked me for my help and left my office for what I thought was to be his last session.

Two months passed before Arnold called me again. He wanted to see me immediately. I cleared some time that evening, and a very unusual journey began. Arnold seemed embarrassed as he told me the following facts out of trance.

People had always dominated him. Everyone from his mother, wife, boss, customers, his children, and just about anyone who had any contact with Arnold dominated him. It was not clear to me what he found especially embarrassing about relating this situation, and when I questioned him, he said he couldn't explain it. It was simply that this fear of being dominated was so strong and made him feel so inferior that he had a lot of trouble expressing it to anyone. In his eighteen years of marriage he had never even discussed this with his wife. Additional sessions were not very fruitful so I suggested the use of simple age regression. Arnold was now willing to try it. I like to obtain as thorough a history as possible out of trance. This relaxes the patient and gives specific paths to explore during actual hypnotic regressions.

When I had worked with Arnold initially, he had obtained a good level of hypnosis easily. Now, simple age regression was difficult for him and his level of trance was light. After some further conditioning, he was finally able to achieve a good medium trance level. We discovered that his childhood was fairly unremarkable, and there were many scenes of his being dominated and manipulated by people in his family as well as by his friends. I was, however, unsuccessful in eliciting a cause for this situation.

I suggested past life regression to Arnold. He was excited by the idea. The first few attempts resulted in very sketchy scenes, and none of them related to his problem. It was as if he were fighting me. One could deduce that subconsciously Arnold was afraid of my dominating him also. A series of four past life regressions made Arnold much more comfortable with the technique and more trusting of me.

Finally one afternoon in November, Arnold described a most unusual past life. This was a very long session and much time had been devoted to establishing the background of the scene.

Arnold's name was Thayer, and he lived in a small village in Bavaria in 1132. Bavaria was part of present-day Germany. He seemed very frightened about something as I questioned him.

Dr. G.:   Where are you?
Arnold: I'm under the table.
Dr. G.:   What are you doing under the table, Thayer?
Arnold: I'm eating my supper.
Dr. G.:   Why are you eating under the table instead of sitting down at the table and placing your food on top of the table?
Arnold: The chains are too short and anyway I'm not allowed to eat that way.
Dr. G.:   What chains?
Arnold: My hands and feet are chained to the table and the chains are very short.
Dr. G.:   Who chained you to the table?
Arnold: Gustave.
Dr. G.:   Who is Gustave?
Arnold: He is my master. I am his apprentice.

Thayer was an apprentice for a master guildsman by the name of Gustave. They worked with metal, mostly silver and gold. Drinking cups, plates, ornaments and various other items for wealthy nobleman were produced by them. During the Middle Ages it was quite common to learn a particular trade by being an apprentice for many years to a master guildsman. What was becoming rather evident was the fact that there was more to this relationship than merely a guildsman and his apprentice.

Dr. G.:   How long have you been chained to the table?
Arnold: Since we closed the shop.

Dr. G.:   Why are you chained this way?

Arnold: I am always chained after the shop is closed. Master Gustave doesn't want me to leave and this is the only way he knows to make sure I don't leave.

Dr. G.:   Why don't you just leave when he unchains you tomorrow?

Arnold: I can't do that. I was apprenticed to him by my father when I was 13.

Dr. G.:   How does Gustave treat you in general?

Arnold: He hates me. He beats me with a whip whenever I do anything wrong. I am afraid of him.

Dr. G.:   Has he always treated you this way?

Arnold: Yes. Ever since I can remember he has always beat me and treated me like this.

Dr. G.:   What happens when customers enter the shop? Does he mistreat you in front of other people?

Arnold: Oh yes, all the time. There's nothing I can do about it. I think he gets great satisfaction out of humiliating me.

Dr. G.:   Is there anyone in particular that Gustave likes humiliating you in front of?

Arnold: Well, yes. There's this girl by the name of Clotilde. He likes to let her see me being treated this way.

Dr. G.:   Who is Clotilde?

Arnold: She is a very nice girl from a wealthy family and she likes me. She has bought many things from Master Gustave. He doesn't like it when she asks about me.

Dr. G.:   What does Gustave do when Clotilde asks about you?

Arnold: He yells at me and tells me I'm worthless. He makes fun of everything I do and say. Then after she leaves, he chains me to the table and beats me.

Dr. G.:   What else does he do to you?

Arnold: Well, he does these unnatural things to me. . . .

Arnold was very embarrassed about this particular question. He started to stutter and after about ten minutes he described a number of homosexual acts that Gustave subjected him to. Gustave had never married and he used Thayer (Arnold) to satisfy his every desire. Thayer was blamed for anything that went wrong. He was degraded by Gustave whenever the latter felt like abusing him. The hatred Thayer and Gustave felt for each other grew daily.

I progressed Thayer to a significant event in his life.

Dr. G.:   Can you tell me what is happening now, Thayer?

Arnold: I, I am scared.

Dr. G.:   Why are you afraid?

Arnold: Master Gustave, he is very angry with me.

Dr. G.:   Why is that unusual?

Arnold: It's not just his usual temper. It's more than that.

Dr. G.:   Why? What has happened since I last spoke with you?

Arnold: Clotilde has shown a great interest in me. She has asked Master Gustave to allow me to do some work at her family's house.

Dr. G.:   How did Gustave respond to that request?

Arnold: He almost lost his temper in front of Clotilde. Her family has given Master Gustave much business over the years, and this is the first time that he has acted this way in front of her. I just know that he is going to beat me tonight.

Dr. G.:   What did Gustave tell Clotilde?

Arnold: He said that I couldn't go to their home because of the tools that I would need, and he told Clotilde that I couldn't be trusted. Imagine, telling Clotilde that. I hate him so.

Dr. G.:   Alright, Thayer, I want you to detach yourself from this scene and move forward to a resolution of this problem on the count of five. One . . . two . . . three . . . four . . . five.

Arnold: I'm being chained to the table again.

Dr. G.:   Is it dinnertime now?

Arnold: Yes, Somehow I feel strange. It's as if I have some extra energy. Master Gustave tells me that he is going to abuse me tonight. He often tells me that before I eat to taunt me.

Dr. G.:   Tell me what happens next, Thayer.

Arnold: I don't let him chain me to the table. I'm arguing with him and he's laughing at me. Why does he laugh at me?

Dr. G.:   What do you do about it?

Arnold: I attack him as he tries to chain my leg to the table.
            The food gets thrown on the floor and Gustave is
            yelling at me. I fight with him and all I can think of
            is killing him. (Patient is very excited.)
Dr. G.:   Now calm down and slowly tell me what is happening.
Arnold: We are on the floor and I am reaching for his throat.
            I want to strangle him. We knocked over some tools
            and something is pressing against my leg.
Dr. G.:   What is it?
Arnold: It's a very sharp tool. I reached down with my left
            hand and brushed it aside but I shouldn't have done
            that.
Dr. G.:   Why not?
Arnold: Master Gustave, he pushed me off of him and punched
            me in the face. I don't know what's happening now.
Dr. G.:   Focus your mind on this scene, Thayer. It's important.
Arnold: He threw me against the wall and cursed me. He said
            I was not worth the trouble I was causing.
Dr. G.:   What does Gustave do next?
Arnold: He picked up a knife-like tool. I know that it's very
            sharp. Oh, my God, he's stabbed me in my stomach.
            (Patient is very excited.) I'm bleeding and the pain is
            unbearable.
Dr. G.:   Relax, Thayer. Detach yourself from any pain or
            emotion and tell me what happens next.
Arnold: He stabbed me many times. I dropped to the floor and
            died. He killed me. That horrible fiend killed me.
Dr. G.:   How do you feel now?
Arnold: I feel as if I'm floating. I can see my body beneath me
            but I can't feel anything.

Since Arnold was upset by this scene, I allowed him to view
his death and to experience the complete detachment from all
discomfort that typically characterizes death scenes. He stayed
with this tranquil scene for about ten minutes. I then brought
him to the superconscious mind level and asked him about
Gustave and Clotilde. He reported to me that Clotilde was his
sister-in-law Margaret, with whom he gets along very well today.
Gustave was not yet involved in his present life.

After this fateful session, Arnold felt much better about himself. He finally realized why he was so afraid of people dominating him and why he seemed to allow other people to exert their influence on him. What is interesting to note is that his sister-in-law Margaret was one of the few people that Arnold has known that has not tried to dominate him. Margaret, as Clotilde, was the only bright spot in Thayer's life.

I saw Arnold a few more times to help him work out his remaining doubts. He was not interested in finding out about other lifetimes in which he might have known Gustave. Arnold felt he had learned enough about his past.

During the next six months, Arnold kept in touch with me. He had made great progress in strengthening his self-image and no longer feared people or allowed them to dominate him. He received a promotion at the store and his relationship with his wife and children had also improved noticeably. I was gratified with the results.

A year and a half after my treatment of Arnold, I received a call from an attorney named Brian, who wanted to work out some psychological problems using hypnosis. Brian specialized in corporate law for a large Baltimore law firm. He was a very successful man in his late thirties, but he felt he had an undesirable tendency to manipulate people. Out of trance he described himself as a self-made man who used people time and time again. It is ironic that the ability to manipulate people, which some consider an asset to an attorney, should be this patient's chief complaint.

Brian's conscience was working overtime. He felt guilty about his actions. Insomnia was a nightly occurrence, along with a compulsive eating problem. I also learned that his hobby was collecting antiques, mostly metal objects such as silverware, drinking cups, jewelry, and so on. He didn't care much for antique furniture. I noted this in his chart for future reference.

Brian proved to be an excellent hypnotic patient. He attained a good trance level and was easy to work with. Some progress was made with his compulsive eating habits and insomnia, but I was not satisfied with the results. I suggested age regression, and after I had thoroughly explained the process to him, Brian agreed to try this technique.

Simple age regression was helpful but not to the extent that I had hoped. Brian relived a number of scenes concerning compulsive eating from his childhood and adolescence, though nothing of importance was discovered concerning his manipulative tendencies. He did report scenes in his adolescence and college years in which he used people for selfish purposes. Yet, I was not satisfied with this data because deeply rooted causes were not surfacing.

Brian couldn't understand my dissatisfaction. He felt he was making progress. I explained to him at this time the use of past life regression and asked him if he would consent to try it. He was skeptical about the concept of past lives but agreed nonetheless.

In late March I brought Brian back into a most interesting past life. He went into trance quickly and deeply and the following represents excerpts from this session:

Dr. G.:   What do you see now?
Brian: I'm working in my shop.
Dr. G.:   What kind of shop is this?
Brian: I'm some sort of metal worker—yes, I'm a master craftsman and I'm damn good at my work.
Dr. G.:   What year is this?
Brian: 1130.
Dr. G.:   What is your name?
Brian: I'm called Gustave.
Dr. G.:   Can you describe your shop?
Brian: Well, it's not a very big shop. I have many fine tools that I use in my work.
Dr. G.:   What specifically do you make?
Brian: I mostly work with gold and silver. Noblemen commission me to make ornaments, jewelry, eating utensils, goblets, decorative containers and other such objects.
Dr. G.:   Are you married?
Brian: No, I don't have the time or patience for women.
Dr. G.:   What country do you live in?
Brian: My land is called Bavaria.
Dr. G.:   Who is the leader of your land?
Brian: King Henry.

Dr. G.:   Do you enjoy your work?

Brian: Yes, I am the best at what I do and I like my craft.

Dr. G.:   Do you speak with the noblemen often?

Brian: Only when they come into my shop.

Dr. G.:   What do they talk about?

Brian: Oh, some damn nonsense about the election of the new Pope.

Dr. G.:   Can you tell me more about the situation?

Brian: Well, not really. I don't get involved with other people's problems. I have enough of my own.

Dr. G.:   What have you heard lately about the Pope?

Brian: The Pope died recently and there is some sort of fight going on as to who will be the next Pope.

Dr. G.:   What kind of fight?

Brian: There were two Popes chosen and nobody knows who is going to remain as Pope. In all my years I have never heard of such dealings. I don't like to think about those things.

An interesting historical note: in the year 1130, Lothair II was the Holy Roman Emperor, and his son-in-law, Henry the Proud, was Duke of Bavaria. Pope Honorius II died in 1130 and two elections were held. A small body of cardinals elected Innocent II while the majority of cardinals elected Analectus II. The latter controlled the Vatican and the castle of S. Angelo. Innocent II was recognized by all of the kings north of the Alps and in Rome as the true Pope. He retired and went with Lothair to Germany until 1136 when Lothair reinstated him as the one and only Pope.

Dr. G.:   Is there anything about your work that you don't like?

Brian: It's my damn, incompetent apprentice.

Dr. G.:   Tell me about your apprentice.

Brian: There's not much to tell. I took this young lad into my shop and tried to make a craftsman out of him. But, he doesn't seem to be able to do the work.

Dr. G.:   What is his name?

Brian: Thayer.

At this point my skin began to crawl. However, my obligation was to my current patient, and it was important to continue this regression as if nothing unusual had happened. After all, Brian knew nothing of Arnold.

Dr. G.:   What exactly does Thayer do that bothers you?
Brian: He exists. That bothers me. I don't know what it is about him but I don't like him. I seem to want to hurt him. He is an incompetent and will never be the master craftsman that I am.

It was significant that Brian lacked this oversized ego in his present life. Although he was unquestionably independent and successful, he was almost soft-spoken and never exhibited such self-importance. In his life as Gustave, he was coarse, crude, cruel, and sadistic. His voice was deeper than Brian's and he spoke much more rapidly.

Dr. G.:   How do you treat Thayer?
Brian: Ha, Ha! You ask a very interesting question. I am too kind to the lad. I feed him, clothe him, and beat him. I am a good provider.
Dr. G.:   You beat him?
Brian: You are offended? Of course I beat him. He deserves no better.
Dr. G.:   Do you enjoy beating him?
Brian: Yes. He does anything I ask and I ask a lot. He doesn't like what I ask of him, but I own him.
Dr. G.:   Tell me more of your life.
Brian: I work hard. I get up with the sun and work until the sun goes down. My work is fine. I am a great craftsman. I am a master.

Gustave went on to describe the details of his life. He was a very lonely and disturbed man. People bothered him. It wasn't just Thayer that he didn't like. He didn't like anyone. Cruelty made him feel good. Thayer provided him with companionship and someone on whom he could vent his frustrations.

Chaining Thayer to the table—which Arnold had described to me from Thayer's point of view—was an example of Gustave's cruelty. The chain was purposely made short to make it uncomfortable for Thayer. Even the simple act of eating became a humiliation. Thayer was used, manipulated, dominated, and utterly degraded by Gustave, nor was Gustave shy about describing the homosexual acts he committed with Thayer.

I next progressed Gustave to the year 1135.

Dr. G.:   How is your business these days?

Brian: Business is good thanks to my skill but not thanks to that good-for-nothing apprentice of mine. All he seems to care about is that damn girl.

Dr. G.:   What girl is that?

Brian: That Clotilde.

Dr. G.:   Who is Clotilde?

Brian: She is the daughter of a wealthy nobleman. Her family has been doing business with me for a long time. Imagine that incompetent actually thinks that a nobleman's daughter could actually love a commoner—and an incompetent one at that!

Dr. G.:   Why is that so impossible to imagine?

Brian: Look, I am a master craftsman. If I can't have a noblewoman such as Clotilde, I'll be damned if I'm going to let Thayer have her. I will see to it that she sees him for what he is.

Dr. G.:   And what is that?

Brian: A commoner. A possession of mine, and a rather worthless one at that.

Dr. G.:   Wouldn't you like to be involved with someone like Clotilde?

The response to that question can't be reported. I seemed to have struck a nerve with that question. Apparently Gustave's misanthropy and his homosexual tendencies grew out of his frustration at not being able to socialize with the nobility. This was a feudal society with a strict class system. Master guildsmen were not allowed to marry or consort with noblewomen. To make matters worse, Gustave was physically unattractive and crude. These frustrations, among others, led to Gustave's attitude toward Thayer and Clotilde. He used Thayer as his scapegoat.

I progressed Brian to the resolution of the situation between Gustave and Thayer.

Dr. G.:   What is happening now?

Brian: I'm going to fix that Thayer once and for all.

Dr. G.:	What did he do now?
Brian:	It's that Clotilde. She had the nerve to ask me to let Thayer go to her house for some special work. Why didn't she ask me to go? I am the master, the best. He is just an apprentice!
Dr. G.:	Is that all that's bothering you?
Brian:	No! I came very close to hurting that girl. She got me very mad.
Dr. G.:	Have you ever acted that way before with her?
Brian:	No. Of course not. It's Thayer's fault and I'm going to fix him good.
Dr. G.:	What are you going to do to him?
Brian:	I'm going to feed him very well tonight. Then I'm going to give him the beating of his life.
Dr. G.:	Don't you think that Thayer will sense that something is wrong?
Brian:	I don't care. I just want to beat him until he begs for mercy.
Dr. G.:	On the count of five, move forward to the actual confrontation with Thayer. One . . . two . . . three . . . four . . . five. What do you see now?
Brian:	I'm chaining Thayer to the table. He looks a little strange after I tell him that this will be a night that he will long remember.
Dr. G.:	What happens next?
Brian:	He talks back to me and keeps moving his leg so I can't chain him to the table. That crazy fool jumps me and tries to knock me down.
Dr. G.:	What do you do about it?
Brian:	I laugh at the fool for his futile attempt to hurt me. Then I pick him up and throw him on the table. He knocks over the nice meal I fixed for him. He will regret this night.
Dr. G.:	Where are you now?
Brian:	I'm standing by the table slapping the idiot. He reaches for my throat and tries to strangle me. Now I'm really mad.
Dr. G.:	What happens next?
Brian:	I pick him up again and throw him against the wall. My tools are there and I tease him with a very sharp

knife. He curses me and I lose my temper. I stab him
again and again. It feels good to rid myself of this
incompetent. He is not worth any more trouble. I
killed him and I am glad.

Dr. G.: Where did you stab Thayer?

Brian: First I stabbed him in his stomach and then I stabbed
him in the neck.

I brought Brian back to the present after a few minutes. He
seemed drained from the session, but he was very impressed by
this experience. He didn't want to pursue additional regressions.
Apparently he felt this one exposure was sufficient.

Over the next few months, Brian made considerable progress
in controlling his manipulative and domineering tendencies. He
has since sent numerous referrals to me. I never did tell him of
the case of Arnold and his past life as Thayer. My professional
ethics prevent me from revealing the details of another patient's
case history.

I have already discussed the concept of synchronicity. Suffice
it to say, my exposure to these two regressions was no coincidence.
The odds must be billions to one against such a situation occurring.
The correspondences were nothing short of startling. All the
names, dates, and events matched. The main difference occurs
in the two accounts of the final fight between Thayer (Arnold)
and Gustave (Brian). According to Thayer, he jumps Gustave,
wrestles him to the floor, and is stabbed in the stomach repeatedly
after Gustave throws him against the wall. In Gustave's version,
he picks up Thayer and throws him against the wall and stabs
him in the stomach repeatedly and then in the neck. The only
discrepancy seems to be who first accosts whom, since if the
stomach wounds killed Thayer, he would never know he had
been stabbed in the neck!

Of course, I considered the possibility of fraud. But it seems
clear to me that neither man had anything to gain from a collusion. And if this was some sort of practical joke, I fail to see a
motive. I had never discussed writing this book with either of
them. In fact, it wasn't until October of 1980 that I even considered writing a book. And, it was a year and a half between
the two regressions. Finally, neither of them has ever contacted

me with respect to publishing their cases. I can only think of this as an example of synchronicity.

Many people have asked me whether Arnold and Brian have ever met in this lifetime. The answer is that they have not met in this incarnation and I had no knowledge of their relationship prior to my regressing them. Furthermore, I have no intention of introducing them, for many reasons. First, if they were supposed to meet again to work out their karma, then they would have come into contact with each other long before they met me. Second, I do not attempt to play God with my patients. To introduce these two people, considering their past life history, would affect both of their karmic cycles. If this were meant to be, it would already be out of my control. Third, I would be concerned about Arnold's possible reaction to Brian, and vice versa. Considering the details of the regressions, both could be hostile and violent.

My involvement as the middle man may very well have been a test of my own karmic cycle. It was tempting to introduce these patients to each other. However, this may have done them both more harm than good, physically and psychologically. If they were meant to meet again in this life they would do so without my interference. Perhaps my knowledge of both Brian and Arnold did help me understand the effects they had on each other during the Middle Ages. I did not feel that they would have benefitted at all from their meeting in this lifetime. Perhaps they will meet in this life but it won't be through me. My role in these two cases is complete. My task is to help the patient understand the root causes of his problems through the use of hypnotic regressions so that he or she is rid of mysterious compulsions and can lead a better existence in this lifetime.

Both Arnold's and Brian's lives have, in fact, been significantly improved as a result of hypnotherapy and especially past life regression. Arnold is less afraid and more self-confident; Brian informed me that he had successfully resisted two opportunities to manipulate a new lawyer in his firm. In addition, Brian's insomnia disappeared entirely, and he lost 25 pounds. Since neither of them showed any interest in exploring additional past lives, I can only guess that they did share additional lifetimes since the 12th century and I hope they fulfilled their karmic obligations.

CHAPTER THIRTEEN

ANOREXIA NERVOSA: SELF-PUNISHMENT FOR HER LAST LIFE

Anorexia nervosa is a very dangerous syndrome. It is characterized by a patient literally starving herself to death. The patient considers herself to be very much overweight even though, in reality, she is at her proper weight or slightly underweight. When she looks in the mirror she fantasizes that she sees an overweight figure. I have observed this neurosis in women of all ages and socio-economic backgrounds. Most commonly it affects young, single women of middle-class backgrounds.

There was a case that was reported to me not long ago about a nineteen-year-old girl who read an article in a leading magazine stating that one can never be too rich or too thin. Since this young woman was from a lower middle-class family with little chance of becoming wealthy, she decided that her only hope was to lose weight quickly by starving herself. This sudden weight loss nearly killed her. After a number of hospitalizations and psychotherapy, she realized the futility and danger of her actions and fortunately came to her senses.

I do not treat many cases of anorexia nervosa, but the number of patients calling me with this problem has definitely increased over the past five years. One warm spring afternoon I received a telephone call from a woman by the name of Gina. Gina was a photographer by profession and she sounded in need of help.

It seemed that for the past three months she had literally been afraid to eat. Gina couldn't explain why, but she wanted to starve herself. Her appetite had all but disappeared and it took a great deal of effort to eat any kind of food. She was five feet six inches tall and now weighed only 92 pounds. Her weight had dropped from 120 pounds in just three months.

Gina arrived at my office the following day, immaculately dressed and, except for a rather emaciated figure, very attractive. She spoke almost in a whisper.

Gina described her problem, beginning when she started having a series of nightmares. At first she couldn't remember anything about her dreams but then memories began to surface. Most of the time she would see a very obese man in his thirties. The look on his face and his mere presence would frighten her. Gina didn't know what this meant, but she did know that she was afraid of this man.

My work with past life regression was well known to Gina, since two of her girl friends had been regression patients of mine. She thought that these scenes could be indications of a past life. I agreed with her premise and began to explain the procedure involved in regressing to a past life.

I informed Gina that it might be difficult at first to go back to this lifetime since she had many negative responses to the scenes she saw in her dream state. Since we are in the alpha state (natural hypnosis) when we dream, it is not uncommon for people to have their own past life regressions while they sleep. Unfortunately, most of the scenes that are relived during the dream state are forgotten immediately upon awakening.

Gina was highly intelligent and, although she had little prior knowledge of karma or hypnosis, followed my explanations with ease. Yet, when I asked her, out of trance, about past experiences with nightmares, she had a great deal of difficulty remembering the last time bad dreams had bothered her. She very rarely remembered her dreams, and when she did they were usually meaningless to her. Before the episode that brought her to my office, she had had occasional nightmares, but none of these had affected her the way these recent dreams had.

During Gina's second session, I used simple age regression to take her through various parts of her childhood. She reported scenes of little significance, but this was preparation for her past life regression. Gina was becoming more and more confident of her ability to relax with hypnosis and self hypnosis. I always teach self hypnosis to my patients for this very reason.

The third and fourth sessions were spent taking Gina through two past lives. The scenes and information that she reported to me were of little value as far as her anorexia nervosa was concerned. In one past life Gina was the wife of a Massachusetts farmer in the 18th century. She lived a full life and had no significant weight problems. The second life we explored showed Gina as a seamstress in Philadelphia during the 1850s. Again no weight problems emerged. It seemed that her subconscious mind was fighting me. I gave her some specific suggestions to allow her subconscious mind to relax any inhibitions concerning exploring past life scenes directly relating to her anorexia.

We were both surprised by what Gina reported during her fifth session. I induced Gina into a medium level trance and directed her back into a past life that would explain the origin of her anorexia.

Dr. G.:   Can you tell me what you see?
Gina: I'm at the doctor's.
Dr. G.:   Why are you there? Are you ill?
Gina: No. I'm just getting weighed. My mom sent me here because of my weight.
Dr. G.:   What is wrong with your weight?
Gina: Well, it's high. (Gina's voice had become very deep and she spoke much slower than normal for her.)
Dr. G.:   What does the doctor tell you?
Gina: He tells me that I must lose 30 pounds.
Dr. G.:   How do you feel about that?
Gina: I want to tell him what he can do with those 30 pounds. (Patient very annoyed.)
Dr. G.:   What is your name?
Gina: Edward. Edward Laslow.
Dr. G.:   How old are you, Edward?
Gina: Call me Eddie. (Patient very demanding). I'm 16.
Dr. G.:   What year is this?
Gina: 1906.
Dr. G.:   Where do you live?
Gina: Chicago.

When I asked about her weight, Gina (Edward) squirmed in the recliner. It was as if seeing herself at that weight disgusted her. Further questioning revealed that Eddie had always been overweight, and his well-to-do parents had tried everything they could think of to help him lose weight.

Eddie was rather spoiled and was used to getting what he wanted. He was also quite cruel and got into many fights at school. He seemed to enjoy bullying other children, especially younger ones. As Gina described his activities, she would continue to squirm in my chair.

I next progressed Eddie ahead five years in time. The following information was uncovered over two 45 minute sessions.

Dr. G.:   Where are you now, Eddie?
Gina: I'm working in one of my father's restaurants.
Dr. G.:   What kind of work do you do?
Gina: I'm assistant manager.
Dr. G.:   Do you like your job?
Gina: It's okay. But I'm going to like it better when I get to be manager.
Dr. G.:   Is that going to take long?
Gina: No. In fact, I'm going to see to it that I'm promoted real soon. (Gina had a very sinister look on her face.)
Dr. G.:   How are you going to do that?
Gina: One of the waitresses, Mary, is a real good friend of mine. I am going to arrange for a little show for my father's benefit.
Dr. G.:   What kind of show?
Gina: My father is a real prude. When he finds out that Mary is having an affair with Stan (the manager), he will most certainly fire Stan and I'll be made manager.
Dr. G.:   Why are you so certain your father will fire Stan?
Gina: Because Stan is a married man and, like I told you, my father is a real prude.

Eddie was a very shrewd operator. He had a great deal of influence on Mary since she owed him some money. It was not difficult for Eddie to talk her into staging an affair with Stan. One evening Mary was entertaining Stan at her apartment when they received an unexpected visitor—Eddie's father. Eddie had one of the waiters inform his father about the affair and the restaurateur went to question Mary about this accusation.

Upon entering Mary's apartment, Eddie's father became outraged at Stan and fired him immediately. The following day Eddie was appointed manager of the restaurant. This type of underhanded dealing was to become a trademark for Eddie.

Over the next ten years, Eddie developed quite a reputation. With his father dead, Eddie was now owner of four restaurants in Chicago. At one time he had a partner but this partnership broke up after it became evident that Eddie had cheated his partner out of fifty thousand dollars. Each time Gina described one of these unethical or illegal dealings, she wore a look of disgust.

I next progressed Eddie to the year 1926. This represented the results of three sessions.

Dr. G.:   Eddie, where are you now?

Gina: I'm in my office counting the day's receipts. It's been a good day.

Dr. G.:   I trust the restaurant business has been good to you.

Gina: It's not just the restaurants. Ha, ha! (Patient was laughing now.)

Dr. G.:   What do you mean?

Gina: I run a separate business on the side.

Dr. G.:   What kind of business?

Gina: A speakeasy, what else?

Dr. G.:   How long have you been involved with speakeasies?

Gina: Oh, about five years now.

Dr. G.:   Who do you get your alcohol from?

Gina: Frankie.

Dr. G.:   Who is Frankie?

Gina: He has connections with the Capone mob. I like Frankie. He's my kind of guy.

Dr. G.:   Why is that?

Gina: Frankie kills people who get in his way. He is always straight with me and I like the way he handles his women.

Dr. G.:   How does he handle his women?

Gina: He beats them when they talk back to him. Now, that's the way to treat a dame.

Dr. G.:   Do you beat your women, Eddie?

Gina: Of course I do. I only hit my wife occasionally. But I beat my other women when they deserve it.

Eddie had many affairs and most of them ended violently. He had two different apartments in the city, which were inhabited by his two mistresses. A couple of his former girl friends were killed by one of Frankie's men. One of these girls had tried to blackmail Eddie while the other had been unfaithful to him. If there was one thing Eddie couldn't tolerate, it was a woman going out on him.

It seems, in addition, that Eddie always rewarded himself with food. He would gorge himself with food after sex, after completing business deals, or after doing anything he found pleasurable. He even bragged to me about a food orgy he had in 1924 after successfully arranging the killing of a federal agent who was investigating his speakeasies.

Interestingly, Eddie would not allow his picture to be taken. He may have been afraid of its being used to identify him by the police, though he had no criminal record. My interpretation is that he didn't like seeing his obese figure. All of Eddie's girl friends were thin and beautiful. His wife was also thin and very attractive. Eddie liked surrounding himself with beautiful objects and beautiful people.

I next progressed Eddie to the last day of his life.

Dr. G.:   Eddie, where are you now?
Gina: I'm in my office putting money into my safe.
Dr. G.:   What year is it?
Gina: It's 1928. Where have you been? (Patient quite nervous.)
Dr. G.:   Are you alone?
Gina: Of course I'm alone. Quiet, can you hear that?
Dr. G.:   No. What's happening?
Gina: It's Frankie. He came in through my private entrance.
Dr. G.:   Why is he here?
Gina: He's accusing me of skimming.
Dr. G.:   Have you been skimming money from Frankie and the mob?
Gina: Yes. Wait a minute, he's pulling a gun on me.
Dr. G.:   Where is Frankie now?
Gina: He's standing in front my desk. He's telling me that he'll never have to worry about me skimming again. (Patient now very excited and begins to stutter.)
Dr. G.:   What's happening now, Eddie?
Gina: Frankie, please don't shoot! No, no, ohh! (Gina was motionless for about a minute.)

I progressed Gina forward after she died to find out exactly what happened. Frankie shot Eddie for cheating the mob out of hundreds of thousands of dollars. Gina seemed to be relieved when death finally came to Eddie. It was obviously an end to a most degrading life. I brought Gina back to the present.

We discussed this life in detail. She was very satisfied with her newfound knowledge. I am happy to report that during the next six weeks, she gained 25 pounds and maintain her weight at about 117 pounds. Her anorexia nervosa disappeared almost immediately and, to the best of my knowledge, has not recurred.

There were many interesting principles that Gina's life as Eddie illustrated. First, her viewing scenes of this past life in the dream state brought back the obesity and degeneracy of that incarnation. Gina couldn't deal with this so she decided to starve herself to prevent herself from becoming the obese Eddie Laslow. It was not just Eddie's obesity that horrified Gina. Eddie's complete lack of ethics or morality, his infidelity to his wife, and his criminal involvements all disgusted Gina.

Second, Eddie never allowed his picture to be taken. In this life Gina is a photographer and loves having her own picture taken. In fact, she once worked as a model.

Third, Gina had a fear of guns that she could never explain. Being shot to death by Frankie in her past life left Gina with this phobia, which disappeared shortly after this regression.

Finally, Gina's voice was naturally very soft, but when she spoke as Eddie Laslow, it became deeper and slower. In addition, she showed many facial changes and at times developed an almost sinister appearance when she spoke as Eddie.

Gina's life was greatly affected by her reliving her existence as Eddie Laslow. It may literally have saved her life.

CHAPTER FOURTEEN

ON A CLEAR DAY
YOU CAN SEE TOMORROW:
FUTURE PROGRESSION WITH HYPNOSIS

Whenever I mention progression into future lives in an interview, I know many listeners scratch their heads in disbelief. The future seems to be forbidden territory. We are all taught that the past has occurred, the present is occurring, but the future has yet to occur. Then how could we possibly know it—by whatever means —in the present?

In Chapter 3, I discussed the concept of time. One has to think in abstract terms to understand it. Suppose, for example, that you are in a helicopter above a major highway. You look down and see that traffic is stopped due to an accident. At this time you could radio someone in a car five miles behind the scene of the accident and inform the driver of the upcoming traffic problem. Since you are in a helicopter above the traffic flow, you are actually detached from the scene itself. The car that you are warning is involved with the traffic flow. In a sense you are reading the future to this car. If the driver of that car keeps driving on that highway, he will be involved with the stopped traffic that you are now observing. The helicopter represents another plane, and on a different plane there is no time as we here on Earth (or on the highway, in this analogy) know it.

To continue the analogy, from the helicopter you could also see what the traffic flow is like behind the car that you are talking to. This would represent the past. The traffic ahead of the driver represents the future, and the traffic that the driver is experiencing now represents the present. You are, in effect, reading the past, present, and future from the helicopter. By leaving the earth plane or entering into a hypnotic trance, you can read the past or future without the restrictions that occur in the waking, or Beta, state.

The actual experience of a progression is rather difficult to describe. I have personally conducted thousands of regressions, though only dozens of progressions. Most people are afraid of the future and don't want to be progressed. Also, I have regressed myself into past lives and progressed myself into future lives, so that I can speak of these phenomena from personal experience. In a regression, the scenes can unfold in a logical and orderly fashion. The patient can recall the past in great detail, and these episodes into the past are often most helpful to him or her in terms of understanding present karma and present behavioral problems. A progression, however, is far less stable. It is much more difficult to obtain information. I am attempting to see how a patient's karma will be manifested in the future when I perform progressions. This knowledge can greatly help a patient in his present life.

It seems that when an individual is progressed into the future, he or she may be quickly removed from a particular scene and transferred to another without any instructions from me. There is, of course, absolutely no danger to the patient, but the continuity of the scene may be lost. For example, the patient could be describing a scene in some futuristic city and the next thing they know, the city has disappeared and a desert scene has replaced it. The patient may then describe a third and completely different scene, and act as if nothing unusual has happened.

Unfortunately, there is no reference source that one can utilize to obtain additional information about our future. Psychics don't write books on this subject, if they do future life progressions at all. I know of no other therapist in the country who does progressions. People are as susceptible to progressions as they are to regressions. Progressions, however, do require more conditioning.

Our subconscious minds are programmed to think of the future as being mysterious and inaccessible. Thus, our minds would inhibit a free flow of information and instead present a constant change in scenes. Another possible explanation of the difficulty of extracting information about the future from the subconscious during hypnosis could be a physical one. The subconscious mind is pure energy. It is characterized by a certain electrical frequency and magnetic field. The future might affect this field and frequency in some way and thus result in this instability.

Karma would also be affected by an individual's seeing into their future. Yet, if we weren't supposed to know the future, progression simply wouldn't work. And in some exciting cases, there's no doubt that it does. Some day I expect science, probably quantum physics, to solve this mystery once and for all.

There have been numerous consistent observations made by my patients as to our future during their hypnotic progressions. Since people have reported similar observations independently in trance, I feel it my duty to report them.

As you will see in the cases that follow, during the 21st century, world peace will finally become a reality. Peace will last for 300 years. Earth will undergo major geographical changes; scientific progress will be most evident. In the next century, hunger, greed, jealousy, prejudice, and other negative aspects of society seem to have been almost entirely eliminated.

During the 22nd century, solar power will be incorporated into everyday life. Much advancement in medical science will be evident, especially in the fields of psychology and psychiatry. The life span of the average adult will be increased to about ninety years.

Technological advancements continue in the 23rd century. Transportation systems become almost noiseless and very efficient; nuclear power is used extensively. Sophisticated computers and video equipment are household appliances. Advanced education is emphasized and readily available. Experiments in weather control are meeting with greater success. An average life span of 110 years also characterizes this century.

It is during the 24th century that mankind reverts to some of its earlier mistakes. International political problems recur; a small scale nuclear war results in a reduction of the world's population; there are further geographical changes to the Earth's surface.

The 25th century is characterized by man's ability to control the weather. Androids are used to perform all menial tasks; medicine makes more advances. A major nuclear war results in a tremendous decrease in the population of the world. However, mankind survives and civilization continues to prosper into at least the next century.

Underwater cities, the routine use of lasers in medicine, and sophisticated genetic engineering will characterize the 26th century. Information pills will keep citizens well informed, and one democratic form of world government will insure the rights of all. People will have much leisure time; the average life span will be over 125 years. Sickness and disease will be almost unknown; interplanetary travel will be a top priority and we will make contact with beings from other planets.

There seems to be an almost eerie stillness in the future, more peaceful, with a few exceptions, and more productive.

It is interesting to note the patient's lack of emotion during future progressions. With rare exceptions, the scenes, no matter how horrible, are described with little reaction. Earthquakes, nuclear wars, accidental deaths, and so on, do not seem to bring out the same emotional response during progression as they do during past life regressions. The reason for this is unclear. Yet you will see it repeatedly in the cases that follow.

CHAPTER FIFTEEN

THE FUTURE LIVES OF
OUR TV PERSONALITY

Early in January 1981, Harry Martin called me expressing interest in progressing into the future through the use of hypnosis. He had done so well with past life regression that he wanted to see if it could work "in reverse." After seeing himself as a self-made warehouse owner in the 18th century, a 19th century blind piano player, and an RAF radio operator during World War II, Harry was ready for an entirely different experience. I explained the theory concerning the space-time continuum and he seemed very enthusiastic about attempting a journey into the future.

At our first session, I wanted to establish the validity of this technique. I decided to progress Harry just one week into the future to the WBAL newsroom assignment board to see if he could read news items about events that hadn't occurred yet. This seemed to be a fair test of hypnotic progression and Harry agreed to it wholeheartedly. My next step would be to progress Harry into a future life. All of these session were tape recorded and I gave Harry a copy of these tapes.

On February 2, 1981, Harry began his first trip into the future. I progressed him one week forward, to February 9, 1981, which was a Monday. The technique simply consisted of Harry's reading either from the newsroom assignment board one hour before air time of his broadcast or his reading from the actual script of that day's newscast. (The first fifteen minutes of "Hello Baltimore" consisted of a news update.)

The following are excerpts from this February 2nd session:

Dr. G.: Tell me exactly what you see on the assignment board.
Harry: Plane, and the number 406.

When I asked Harry to read the newscript about this item, this is what he reported:

Harry: State aviation officials are investigating the crash of a light plane this morning near route 406.

This item never made it on the air, but on February 9th a small plane did crash in Bowie, Maryland. This crash was investigated by state aviation officials.

Dr. G.:   What is the next item on the assignment board?
Harry: It's the name of a place, I think, but I can't make it out.
Dr. G.:   Can you spell it?
Harry: It's a long name. It's a very weird combination of consonants. It's the name of a man.
Dr. G.:   What letters can you make out?
Harry: ST W KI . . . it's a long Russian-type name.

On February 9th Stanislaw Kania, Poland's labor leader, was told that he might soon be fired unless he instructed his workers to return to work.

Dr. G.:   Move down to the next item that you will be reading on the air. Tell me what the script says.
Harry: This is an accident. It's on 695 (the Baltimore Beltway) between the Pikesville and Security Boulevard exits, but I don't know where.
Dr. G.:   What vehicles are involved in the accident?
Harry: One large vehicle and one small one. There were no deaths.

On February 9th a school bus on its way to Randallstown (between Pikesville and Security Boulevard) hit a car at 200 Embleton Road in Owings Mills (just north of Pikesville). No deaths were reported.

Dr. G.:   What is the next news item, Harry?
Harry: It has to do with Governor Hughes and the budget.
Dr. G.:   What about the budget?
Harry: Governor Hughes says he's holding the line this year on the budget. The legislature is going against him

for some reason, saying that they don't have to hold the budget on some raise proposal.

On February 12th, Governor Hughes vetoed a $40 to $60 million raise for state employees. The Maryland Classified Employees Association (MCEA) had obtained the support of the State Legislature in voting for a salary raise.

Dr. G.:   What is the next news item?
Harry: It's something about Jerry Falwell.
Dr. G.:   What about Jerry Falwell?
Harry: It has something to do with Falwell's interview that appeared in *Penthouse*.

On February 4th Jerry Falwell withdrew his law suit against *Penthouse* magazine. (Remember, this session was taking place February 2nd.)

Harry's next progression session was the following Monday, February 9th. There was much excitement and enthusiasm in his voice when we discussed last week's "hits." I was also stimulated and elated with the results of the last session.

Anyone can do what Harry accomplished. The hypnotic state allows the psychic component of the brain to be tapped. We all have this progression ability. Naturally, I do not use this technique to predict stock values or lottery numbers. First, I consider this an unethical use of our natural psychic abilities. Second, the dates are not always accurate. A progression of one week in the future may, in actuality, be 3 days or 10 days hence.

I then progressed Harry to February 16th and again had him read the news items on the script that would be used on the air.

Dr. G.:   What news item appears next on the script?
Harry: A fire in the city.
Dr. G.:   What kind of building was involved?
Harry: A house fire; a row house.
Dr. G.:   Do you see the name of the person who owned the house?
Harry: I want to say Johnson. They don't own it, I think they just live there.
Dr. G.:   Anything else?
Harry: There are two little girls involved.

Dr. G.: Are they hurt?

Harry: No, they escaped safely but somebody was hurt. I don't know who, though.

Dr. G.: Can you see anything else?

Harry: I see two little girls being dangled from the second story window of this row house. They're being rescued by someone. They had ribbons in their hair.

On February 13th a child named Kenneth Blanda died in a second-story fire on 540 Pulaski Street in the western part of Baltimore City. A space heater had caused the fire. Patricia Johnson, a neighbor, was interviewed about the fire. This fire did occur in a row house.

What is especially interesting is that in four of the six "hits," the dates matched perfectly. With one of the misses the date was five days before, and with the other it was three days before the predicted date. I consulted with a professor of mathematics at a local university and he stated that the odds were hundreds of thousands to one against this type of thing happening by mere chance. These hits don't *prove* progression but, in my opinion, they lend significant credence to the theory.

The following chart summarizes Harry's progressions:

DATE OF SESSION	NEWS ITEM GIVEN IN TRANCE	ACTUAL NEWS ITEM THAT OCCURRED
February 2, 1981	State aviation officials investigating light plane crash—route 406.	February 9, 1981—A small plane crashed in Bowie, but this item didn't make it on the air.
	ST W KI—Long name with many consonants—possibly a Russian name.	February 9, 1981—Stanislaw Kania, Polish labor leader, may be fired.
	Accident on 695 between Security Blvd. and Pikesville. NO DEATHS.	February 9, 1981—A school bus on its way to *Randallstown* hit a car at 200 Embleton Rd. (Owings Mills) NO DEATHS.
	Harry Hughes (wants to hold the line on the budget) fights	February 12, 1981—Harry Hughes wouldn't approve 40–60 million dollar raise for

	with State Legislature (wants to spend more $).	state employees. Maryland Classified Employees Assn. (MCEA) said salaries should be raised.
	Jerry Falwell— *Penthouse* interview	February 4, 1981—Jerry Falwell withdrew his lawsuit concerning his interview that appeared in *Penthouse*.
February 9, 1981	Fire in the city— row house. The Johnsons live there. A neighbor helped rescue two children from the second story. One child was hurt.	February 13, 1981—Kenneth Blanda (a child) died in a 2nd-story fire on 540 Pulaski St. in west Baltimore. A space heater caused the fire. Patricia Johnson, a neighbor, was interviewed about the fire.

On March 9th, Harry came to my office for a progression into a future lifetime. He was excited about this adventure. I induced him into a medium trance and began questioning him. During this entire session, Harry spoke in a slow, almost monotonous voice, expressing no emotion whatsoever.

Dr. G.: What do you see before you?

Harry: A pyramid.

Dr. G.: Is this pyramid isolated or are there other structures around it?

Harry: It's isolated.

Dr. G.: Where is this pyramid?

Harry: It's in the desert.

Dr. G.: What is the purpose of this pyramid?

Harry: It has something to do with energy. It's getting energy from the sun.

Dr. G.: Are there any other structures by the pyramid that are related to its energy functions?

Harry: There are pipes on the bottom of it.

Dr. G.: Why are you there?

Harry: I'm just observing. It's like a tour.

Dr. G.: How long have you been there?

Harry: I've just arrived.

Dr. G.: How long are you going to be there?

Harry: Another hour and then we're going to leave.

I next progressed Harry to the tour itself.

Dr. G.: What do you see now?

Harry: The pyramid is made of glass.

Dr. G.: Are you inside the pyramid now?

Harry: Yes. There are living quarters in the far corners with plants and all sorts of supplies.

Dr. G.: How tall is the pyramid?

Harry: 70 feet high.

Dr. G.: What is the source of energy for this pyramid other than the sun?

Harry: Nothing.

Dr. G.: How many people live inside the pyramid?

Harry: 300.

Dr. G.: What is the purpose of this pyramid?

Harry: It's a self-sufficient structure. These 300 inhabitants are specially selected scientists.

Dr. G.: What is the name of the pyramid?

Harry: Phobos.

Dr. G.: Can you describe the leader of the tour?

Harry: A man wearing yellow coveralls leads us.

DR. G.: How many of you are on this tour?

Harry: There are 10 of us.

Dr. G.: Can you see any personal effects in this pyramid that would indicate that people are currently living here?

Harry: Yes. There are plants in various quarters.

Dr. G.: What form of communication exists in the pyramid?

Harry: We don't speak. We think and our thoughts are transmitted as images. That is the purpose of this scientific team; to explore silent communication.

Dr. G.: Can you see what the people on the tour are wearing?

Harry: We all wear a one-piece coverall suit of a certain color.

Dr. G.: What kind of footwear do you have on?

Harry: It's a rubber ankle-high boot that's the same color as the suit.

Dr. G.: Does the color of the suit have any meaning?

Harry: Yes. Each color signifies your function and rank on this project.

Dr. G.: What is your color?

Harry: Beige.

Dr. G.:   What colors are the other people on the tour wearing?
Harry: We are all wearing beige. Red is the lowest color. Next
          is beige, orange, yellow, green and violet. As we pro-
          gress in our duties we move on to the higher colors.
Dr. G.:   What do the scientists in the pyramid do as you
          observe them?
Harry: They just seem to be walking back and forth.
Dr. G.:   Do they make any sounds?
Harry: No.
Dr. G.:   What year is this?
Harry: 2153.

I next progressed Harry forward in time to when he will be at
work in his profession.

Dr. G.:   What do you see now?
Harry: I'm outside looking up at the glass pyramid.
Dr. G.:   Is this the same pyramid that you were in when I last
          spoke with you?
Harry: Yes.
Dr. G.:   What is your purpose in being outside now?
Harry: These glass panels have to be kept free of sand in order
          for the pyramid to operate properly. I inspect these
          panels. I make sure these panels are clean.
Dr. G.:   Do you now work and live in the pyramid?
Harry: Yes.
Dr. G.:   Do you have any way of noting down what needs to
          be replaced or corrected?
Harry: No. There's nothing like that. There is no writing.
Dr. G.:   How do you communicate problems with your
          supervisors?
Harry: You think about it and they will know it.
Dr. G.:   Are you the only inspector?
Harry: Yes.

This was Harry's first job in this future lifetime. He had very
little formal training for this inspector position. I next progressed
Harry forward in time by ten years.

Dr. G.:   Where do you find yourself now?
Harry: I'm inspecting the irrigation system.

Dr. G.: Has anything changed since I last spoke with you?

Harry: Yes. The pyramid is now being used for farming purposes.

Dr. G.: Could you elaborate?

Harry: All of the plants are grown in water, not soil. The water has all the necessary nutrients in it.

Dr. G.: What exactly do you do now?

Harry: I help monitor the ratio of various nutrients in the water so that the correct proportions are present.

Dr. G.: Do you do this yourself?

Harry: No, the computer does this. I just double-check the computer.

Dr. G.: What do you do if the computer is malfunctioning?

Harry: I repair it.

Dr. G.: What color is your suit?

Harry: Yellow.

Apparently Harry had been promoted to a much more sophisticated position in the pyramid. I now progressed Harry to the last day of his future life.

Dr. G.: Where are you?

Harry: I'm reporting to the termination room.

Dr. G.: Are you still in the pyramid?

Harry: Yes.

Dr. G.: Why are you in the termination room?

Harry: It's my turn to change units.

Dr. G.: Can you describe this procedure?

Harry: I lie down on a table and they put something on my fingers and you just go to sleep.

Dr. G.: What does this do to you?

Harry: It takes all of your energy out of you.

Dr. G.: Why is this done?

Harry: You can now be placed in a more appropriate unit. You don't grow old or grow up. You are just transferred.

Dr. G.: Is this then a mechanical body?

Harry: No. It's a totally biological unit.

Dr. G.: What happens in between going from one unit to another?

Harry: You are stored on tape.
Dr. G.:   Do you have a choice as to whether or not you will
           enter a certain unit?
Harry: No.

Harry's voice and delivery in answering my questions were particularly interesting to me. I was also fascinated with Harry's report of the experiments in mental telepathy and the use of solar energy as the only energy source fascinated me. The isolation of this future life was similar to Harry's past life as Hap, the blind piano player. Even though he was born blind, Hap exhibited no remorse. As a 22nd century irrigation inspector Harry easily accepted his "termination." The 18th century life as a warehouse owner and director of an import-export business required that he be an inspector and was also lonely work. This karmic lesson still needed to be learned 400 years later.

When Harry received his promotion to irrigation supervisor this reminded me of his start in newscasting as a radio personality. He was then promoted to television reporting. Today Harry is a well organized television newscaster. He acquired this discipline from at least three previous lifetimes. As an RAF radio operator he was well trained in scientific discipline.

Assertiveness is a trait Harry Martin possesses today. It is a necessary quality for a television personality. Yet, during the 19th, 20th (as the RAF radio operator) and 22nd centuries this characteristic was lacking. The karmic lesson was learned and didn't have to be repeated.

Harry's second future lifetime was revealed two weeks later. He came to my office on this spring afternoon feeling quite relaxed. I induced him into a medium trance and proceeded with the questioning.

Dr. G.:   What do you see?
Harry: I see white curtains in front of a window that look like
           lace.
Dr. G.:   What else do you see?
Harry: I'm inside this room and I'm looking at my work.
Dr. G.:   What kind of work is that?
Harry: Silver plates. There are these silver plates on the wall.

Harry's answers were again almost mechanical without any expression of emotion. His speech pattern was very slow and his voice very deep. This was to continue throughout the session.

Dr. G.:   What is characteristic about these plates?
Harry: They have emblems on them but no writing.
Dr. G.:   Can you describe the furniture?
Harry: The design of the couch and chairs is cubical.
Dr. G.:   What is this place?
Harry: It's my home.
Dr. G.:   What is special about this particular day?
Harry: This is a rest day.
Dr. G.:   What kind of work do you do?
Harry: I'm a sort of a craftsperson.
Dr. G.:   What do you construct?
Harry: Those plates. Those silver plates on the wall.
Dr. G.:   Who do you do these for?
Harry: People. People request my services.
Dr. G.:   Are there many craftsmen like you?
Harry: No. There are only a few of us who do this kind of work.
Dr. G.:   What do people call you?
Harry: Amygdala.
Dr. G.:   Is that your complete name?
Harry: Yes.
Dr. G.:   What year is this?
Harry: 2271.

I next progressed Amygdala forward in time by two years.

Dr. G.:   Can you tell me more about your work?
Harry: These plates are made of silver. They are a means of currency.
Dr. G.:   Are there other forms of currency?
Harry: Yes. You see, these silver plates are a way of holding massive amounts of wealth.
Dr. G.:   The fact that you have some of these silver plates on your wall, does that mean that you are wealthy?
Harry: Yes.
Dr. G.:   Why do people come to you for your work? Why don't they just store their own silver?

Harry: What happens is my making these plates increases the value of the metal.

Dr. G.:   What kind of work do some of your clients do?

Harry: Law, and some of my people are in manufacturing and transportation.

Dr. G.:   What kind of transportation are you referring to?

Harry: Molecular reassembly. This type of transportation is new but is being used more and more.

Dr. G.:   Are there any other uses for molecular reassembly?

Harry: Sustenance. We have small units that help nourish us while we sleep.

Dr. G.:   Could you describe your own molecular reassembly unit?

Harry: It's a platform, a round platform. There is a coordinate tracking system to set it.

Dr. G.:   Do you need someone else to activate it?

Harry: No.

Dr. G.:   When you do use it, how do you get reassembled?

Harry: It's programmed into the unit by the tracking system.

Dr. G.:   Can you describe the last time you used the molecular reassembly unit for transporting yourself?

Harry: I recently went into the city for a meeting.

Dr. G.:   Was anyone else present?

Harry: There were two other people. One is a man dressed in a gray suit made of very shiny material. (Patient paused.)

Dr. G.:   And the woman, how was she dressed?

Harry: Oh, I'm really confused. (Patient exhibited emotions for the first time since the session began.)

Dr. G.:   Why are you confused?

Harry: How did you know it was a woman?

Dr. G.:   You said one of these two people was a male, so I assumed that the other was female. How was she dressed?

Harry: This other person in the room is not really a woman.

Dr. G.:   Is she human?

Harry: Partially. She is part human and part machine.

Dr. G.:   Can you describe her?

Harry: The top half of her body is of human form but the
          way she gets around is by machine. Her head is shaved.
          Her eyes are slanted and her skin is very pale.

It seemed the lower part of this being consisted of a mech-
anized apparatus similar to a wheelchair.

Dr. G.:   Is there anyone else in the room?
Harry: No, just the computer.
Dr. G.:   What is the purpose of this meeting?
Harry: It has something to do with insurance.
Dr. G.:   Personal insurance or work-related insurance?
Harry: Work related.
Dr. G.:   Can you read the policy right now?
Harry: There's no writing. You plug it in. (Patient sounded
          bored.)

I next progressed Amygdala to the time that he would return
home and review his policy.

Dr. G.:   What are you doing now?
Harry: I'm plugging the policy into the wall. The screen asks
          for my ID number so that only I can review it.
Dr. G.:   What specifically does it state?
Harry: Amygdala . . . insured against defects in workmanship.
          Mars 1522.

Amygdala didn't know what Mars 1522 referred to. I returned
Harry to the present.

In this life Harry (Amygdala) showed more of his creative
potential as the silver craftsman. This society seemed to value
silver more than any other metal and crime was almost unknown.
In his present life, Harry is also quite creative. He is currently
writing a novel, plays the drums, and is much involved with the
production aspect of a news mini-series. As the 19th century piano
player Hap, Harry was also showing his creativity. The RAF radio
operator died before he could leave his mark on society. Harry's
career as a television personality is his way of contributing to the
world. This 23rd-century life was the culmination of at least 400
years of creative talent. The great wealth that Amygdala accumu-

lated, in addition to the recognition he was shown, were karmic paybacks for centuries of hard work and dedication.

In the 1980s Harry is well on his way to "doing his thing." He has learned from his past and future lives the value of creativity and recognition. Now, as a media personality, he can put these lessons to use. Of the many benefits he received from hypnotherapy, Harry states that focusing his concentration, acquiring more discipline and energy, and the realization that maybe he should start loving life (taking time to smell the roses, and so on) were most significant. Developing a more open attitude toward hypnotherapy and a better understanding of himself must be added to these advantages. Perhaps the knowledge that there will still be a world in 300 years is enough to give us all an optimistic view of the future.

My reaction to Harry's progressions and regressions was one of satisfaction. Harry has previously stated positive changes in his behavior and attitude toward life. These positive results make me feel proud to be a hypnotherapist.

Most patients don't want to know about the future. That is unfortunate because of the tremendous therapeutic potential progression represents. Whether you believe in progression, regression, or hypnosis doesn't really matter. Anyone can obtain the benefits Harry Martin received through hypnotherapy.

CHAPTER SIXTEEN

MARSHA: A CAREER WOMAN OF THE FUTURE

Nancy, a 34-year-old waitress in a small Baltimore restaurant, first came to me for a past-life regression. In one of her past lives she was a cleaning woman in a Madrid hotel during the 19th century. She worked very hard to put her son (her daughter in this life) through school. One night she was raped and suffered much indignation from the hotel manager (her former husband in this life). Another past-life regression revealed Nancy as a beggar in Italy during the 14th century. After a number of additional successful regressions, we discussed the idea of progression. She was very interested and I arranged to progress her into a future lifetime on her next appointment.

Nancy had no background in parapsychology. She had never read books on the topic. She had little formal education. Her interests in this field began when she saw me interviewed on television. She had been divorced for seven years and had been the victim of much harassment from her former husband, yet she was not bitter. Rather, she was always pleasant and cooperative.

On a Wednesday afternoon at the end of October, this personable young woman began her trip into the twenty-third century. Nancy entered into a hypnotic trance quickly. In a matter of minutes she was in a deep trance and ready to respond to my questions. When I instructed her, she went right into a future life, as if it were something she did every day. This is what we discovered from these taped sessions.

Dr. G.:   What do you see at this moment?

Nancy: I, I'm not sure. I seem to be floating. I can't make anything out.

Dr. G.: Focus on my voice. On the count of three you will no longer be floating. One . . . two . . . three. Now can you tell me what you see?

Nancy: I'm on my way to the Ministry.

Dr. G.: What Ministry is that?

Nancy: The Ministry of Peace, of course. My training is almost complete and I'm very excited about my career.

Dr. G.: What year is this?

Nancy: Why it's 2206.

Dr. G.: What is your name?

Nancy: Marsha.

Dr. G.: How long have you been with the Ministry?

Nancy: Four years. In a few months I will be given my first assignment. I'm so excited. This is what I've wanted to do ever since I was a child.

Marsha's voice was childlike as she described this scene. Yet her vocabulary was sophisticated and she seemed to express more emotions than she did as Nancy.

Dr. G.: How old are you, Marsha?

Nancy: I'm twenty-four.

Dr. G.: What nation is the Ministry of Peace associated with?

Nancy: Why, we are a member of the Western Federation of Nations. You must be new to our country.

Dr. G.: How do your parents feel about your work?

Nancy: Oh, they are very proud of me. I am an only child and my parents want me to do what I want.

Dr. G.: What are your parents' names and what do they do?

Nancy: My mother's name is Lani and she is a housewife now. She used to be an architect. My father's name is Howard and he is a nuclear engineer.

Dr. G.: Who trains you at the Ministry of Peace?

Nancy: Most of our training is done by the simulators (a self-teaching video cassette). We go along with the diplomats after certain phases of our training are complete. We must first pass some rather comprehensive examinations.

In a calm, monotone voice, Nancy (Marsha) described an ultra-modern city. The sidewalks moved along as if one were on a conveyor-belt or an escalator that moved horizontally. Most of the buildings were white and very tall. The streets were immaculately clean and smooth, almost marble-like. There was very little noise to distract people. The two major forms of transportation were the monorail above ground and a kind of subway. There were no cars permitted inside the city limits. Thus, there was virtually no pollution and no vehicle accidents. Even the monorail, subway, and moving sidewalks operated with only the slightest amount of noise. It seemed that this society had conquered noise as well as air pollution.

The average life span was about 110 years. Mandatory retirement was set at age 85.

The lack of stability that I have previously alluded to during progressions was illustrated by the next conversation. Since this information was reported haphazardly and out of sequence, I have pieced together the story of this 23rd-century career woman.

Dr. G.: Marsha, can you tell me more about your work?
Nancy: As I mentioned before, I work for the Ministry of Peace in the Diplomatic Core. In a few months my training will be completed and if I pass my exams, I will be given my first assignment. I am very. . . .

All of a sudden she stopped talking and remained motionless and relaxed in her chair.

Dr. G.: Marsha, where are you now?
Nancy: I'm in the jungle. It's so hot and humid.
Dr. G.: Where is this jungle located?
Nancy: It's in Brazil, not far from the Amazon River. I'm with the Diplomatic Corps on assignment.
Dr. G.: What year is this?
Nancy: 2207.

Nancy had progressed herself forward one year in time. She was sweating even though my therapy room was about 70 degrees. At this time Marsha was on assignment in Brazil. It seemed that weather experiments conducted by the Western Federation accidentally had created a small earthquake which had destroyed a number of small towns in this area, and the Western Federation had sent Marsha and two other diplomats to work out the details of the financial assistance and to smooth things out politically. Marsha didn't know much about these experiments but it seemed that the Federation was attempting to regulate the weather through the use of high-pitched sound. Brazil was a member of the Western Federation, along with North America, the rest of South America, Central America, Western Europe, Africa, and the Middle East.

Dr. G.: Marsha, can you tell me what is happening now?

Nancy: My superior is working out the details of the mission with the Brazilian representative. I am filming the disaster site.

Dr. G.: Why are you meeting in the jungle instead of in an embassy?

Nancy: Federation regulations require us to investigate the site of the catastrophe. We must bring back videotapes of the affected area.

Dr. G.: Is this your first assignment?

Nancy: Oh, heavens no. I've been on six other assignments in the past nine months.

Dr. G.: What is happening now?

Nancy: I seem to be . . . I'm at my desk writing up reports of the Brazilian catastrophe.

Apparently, Marsha departed from the jungle scene and returned to the Ministry of Peace. She had progressed herself two weeks forward in time. I next progressed Marsha forward to a scene outside of the Ministry.

Dr. G.: What is the weather like outside?

Nancy: It is sunny and warm. The S.D.'s are going to have to work overtime today.

Dr. G.: What are S.D.'s?

Nancy: Why, they're solar discs, of course. It's really quite pretty to see them move like that.

Further questioning revealed that these solar discs were large structures that slowly rotated in wide arcs. They were responsible for heating and cooling the city as well as providing other energy needs. I then progressed Marsha to her living quarters. She lived in an apartment in the city.

Dr. G.: Marsha, can you describe your apartment to me?

Nancy: Well, I live on the ninth elevation. What exactly do you want to know?

Dr. G.: How is your food prepared?

Nancy: My apartment is fully equipped with an omni-regulator.

Dr. G.: What is an omni-regulator?

Nancy: It is a self-regulating cooking unit that prepares all forms of consumables to my pre-programmed specifications.

Dr. G.: How do you communicate with other people from your apartment?

Nancy: I use my view-phone.

Dr. G.: What does the view-phone do?

Nancy: It is a device that I speak into. There is a small screen attached to it that allows me to see the person calling me. We use devices of this type at the Ministry for security purposes, only those are far more complex.

Dr. G.: Can you describe anything else in your apartment that operates by mechanical devices?

Nancy: The doors and windows are equipped with electronic devices that control their opening and closing. These devices are programmed to respond to certain words. By repeating these words or phrases I can open or close them without getting up.

Dr. G.: Can you tell me more about your work at the Ministry?

Nancy: I am not cleared to discuss that many aspects of my position, but I will try to be as informative as possible.

Dr. G.: Didn't you say that your Ministry is part of the Western Federation of Nations?

Nancy: That's correct.

Dr. G.: What other great nations exist at this time?

Nancy: There are no great nations, just the Alliance.

Dr. G.: What is the Alliance?

Nancy: The Eastern Alliance includes all those countries that aren't a member of the Western Federation of Nations.

Russia, China, India, Japan, Southeast Asia, New Zealand, Australia, and some smaller islands, along with parts of Eastern Europe were included in the Eastern Alliance. However, there didn't seem to be any ill feelings between the Western Federation and the Eastern Alliance. The main differences were philosophical. There hadn't been any wars in over 100 years. Marsha was then progressed to the year 2221.

Dr. G.:   What do you see now?

Nancy: I'm in my office. My work schedule is very congested.

Dr. G.:   Why is that?

Nancy: There are many problems with the Eastern Alliance.

Dr. G.:   What specifically is the problem?

Nancy: The Ministry received a request from India to act as an arbitrator in a local border dispute. The problem arose when the message was misplaced by one of our computer banks and no response was sent. The Indian delegation then sent a similar request to the Eastern Alliance. Last week our computer gave us the message and we immediately sent a team down to India. Now there are two groups of arbitrators, and there is no protocol to decide who should stay and who should leave.

Dr. G.:   Why wouldn't India have gone to the Eastern Alliance first?

Nancy: India is not happy with the Alliance and has been trying to join the Federation for years.

Dr. G.:   What is your present position with the Ministry?

Nancy: I'm head of the Arbitration Division of Section C-311.

Dr. G.:   What does that entail?

Nancy: I am a supervisor over 47 arbitrators. These arbitrators handle small negotiations which I assign to them. If there are problems or if there is an unusual situation, then I might handle it myself.

Dr. G.:   Then, you mostly stay in the Ministry rather than being out in the field?

Nancy: That's correct. I prefer to go out on missions every now and then as a change of pace.

Dr. G.:   Are you married now?

Nancy: No. I have devoted my life to the Ministry. I love my work.

Dr. G.:   Do you date often?

Nancy: Not very often. I am not seeing anyone at this time, but that doesn't bother me.

Dr. G.: What do you like to do when you are not working?

Nancy: I get a great deal of satisfaction from my vegetations (plants).

As I was questioning Marsha, she suddenly transported herself to a large meeting room in the Ministry of Peace. It seemed that she was going over her notes alone in this large room. This was just a few hours ahead in time from her last answer to my question concerning her outside interests. This particular hypnotic session was rather long (about an hour and a half), and the frequency of switching scenes became less of a problem during the last half hour of this trance. I began questioning her about her interests again.

Dr. G.: Do you ever go to the theater?

Nancy: Yes, but not very often.

Dr. G.: What plays are currently running in New York?

Nancy: New York? I don't understand. Where is New York?

Dr. G.: Isn't there a city called New York that is known for its theater?

Nancy: Oh, you must be referring to New City. There was such a place called New York, but that city was destroyed by the great earthquake over 150 years ago. The city was completely destroyed and it took many years to rebuild it. It was renamed New City. I haven't heard the name New York mentioned since I was in school many years ago studying history.

Dr. G.: Is New City still a theater center?

Nancy: Well, not really. After it was rebuilt, if I can remember my history, theater became more universal and no single city became the permanent seat or main contributor to this field. New City functioned just like any other city.

Dr. G.: Were there any other cities that were destroyed by the great earthquake?

Nancy: Yes, a number of smaller cities were also destroyed. San Francisco and Los Angeles were leveled just before

New York collapsed. It seemed funny to me that both
San Francisco and Los Angeles retained their names
when they were rebuilt, but New York was renamed
New City.

When Marsha spoke of the great earthquake, she showed
complete emotional detachment. This destruction apparently
had little meaning to her. What had occurred in the past was
almost forgotten. The only things that seemed important to
Marsha were her activities at the Ministry and her vegetations.

I next progressed Marsha to the year 2235, in which she was
53 years old. She described a very full life, being active in athletics
and community affairs. She seemed to function like a 20th-cen-
tury woman in her late twenties or early thirties. Her vegetations
were still important to her. There were no wars or other catastrophies to report during the past fourteen years, and the Eastern
Alliance got along famously with the Western Federation. Marsha had become head of the entire arbitration division of the
Ministry of Peace, not just Section C-311. It was not unusual for
women to attain high governmental positions. As a result, there
was apparently no feminist movement or any other kind of
movement; there simply wasn't a need. Mankind had apparently
learned to live peacefully; prejudice, jealousy, greed, hunger,
and fear were all but extinct. When problems did occur, they
were handled quickly and efficiently.

Television, computers, and other electronic marvels were commonplace. People were informed about current events constantly; sickness was a rare phenomenon. What I found most
interesting was the lack of psychological problems. Citizens of the
23rd century didn't seem to get anxious or depressed. Tran-
quilizers were not needed. Communication problems rarely
manifested themselves. This had a direct effect on politics (making
Marsha's job much easier).

When I brought Nancy back to the present, she felt relaxed
and good about her experiences. She found them difficult to
accept, but gradually she admitted the possibility of a future life
as Marsha.

There were a number of interesting elements in this session.
First Nancy's voice deepened and her speech slowed considerably

when she spoke as Marsha. Most notably, her vocabulary increased tremendously. Nancy was shocked by the command she had of language in trance. Third, she behaved more confidently as Marsha. Marsha was very proud of her achievements and talked about little else outside of Ministry affairs. Nancy, on the other hand, never talked about her job as a waitress and spent many hours with her friends and her daughter. Nancy was married at the age of seventeen, but Marsha never married. Clearly, there were great differences between Nancy and Marsha—perhaps due in part to the improved social status of women in this future society.

Nancy's position in society during her past lives was rather low on the socio-economic scale. As a waitress in this life she hadn't made much progress in her station in life. By viewing her future as a successful careerwoman with the Ministry of Peace Nancy sensed that she not only could, but would improve her professional status. As Marsha, she accepted a very responsible position and devoted her life to the Ministry. I noted how proud she acted after seeing this future life.

Karma was at work here as well. The close relationship that existed between Nancy and her daughter was exemplified during the 19th century in Madrid when Nancy worked hard as a cleaning woman to put her son (her daughter in this life) through school. In addition, the degradation showed her by the manager of this hotel in Spain (her ex-husband in her present life) carried over as harassment by him even after their divorce in this life. The lessons of a close family life were learned and, as Marsha, she no longer required a close family unit to achieve her goals. Her career dominated her life in the 23rd century.

CHAPTER SEVENTEEN

ZEKU: A CASE OF GENETIC ENGINEERING

Progressions into future lifetimes are characterized by two unusual events. The first is that the patient will usually regress into a past life before progressing forward into a future life. The second is the lack of stability of scenes I have already described. It doesn't seem to matter whether these are positive, negative or neutral scenes; they will appear and disappear suddenly. During this time the patient remains very relaxed. Many scenes appear cloudy and background sounds are evident to the patient and sometimes distracting. High-pitched sounds and repetitious thumping noises are commonly reported, but they disappear quickly.

Larry was a skeptic about hypnosis in general. He called me three years ago to inquire about my hypnosis practice. A friend of his wife's had been regressed by me into a number of past lives, and Larry had been arguing with her about it for over a year. He made it quite clear to me that he thought this entire field was pure fantasy, without any scientific substance. Larry was articulate about his skepticism and he ended the conversation by asking me if I would consider regressing him under these conditions.

I like challenges. The idea of successfully regressing Larry appealed to me, not because I thought it would alter his opinion much, but because I like difficult cases. Larry came across to me as a very logical thinker. His professional calling involved the management of many employees in a large Baltimore corporation. His work was very high-pressured, and he was a very unemotional man. When I asked him why he bothered to argue so much with his wife's friend, he stated that he didn't like illogical and unscientific philosophies.

The argumentative and hypercritical characteristics illustrated by Larry are far from ideal for hypnosis, but I accepted the challenge. In April I regressed Larry back into his childhood. I was happily surprised to find that Larry was an excellent hypnotic patient. To show him the positive effects of hypnosis, I gave him some motivational suggestions to help him in his high-pressured job. These suggestions worked quickly and well. It didn't take Larry long to see the benefits and validity of hypnosis, but he was still skeptical about past lives.

We began Larry's journey into his previous lives in early May. The first two past life regressions were sketchy, but Larry's interest was increasing and his skepticism was diminishing. After two additional past life regressions, he was warming considerably to the idea. There were many karmic lessons that were applicable to his present life, and his recognition of their significance resulted in some major improvements in his personal and professional life. One of these regressions dealt with Larry in a past life as a merchant in England during the 16th century. He was argumentative, stubborn, and narrow-minded in that life and this resulted in an early and violent death. One day he argued with a customer so strongly that this shopper strangled Larry. Now he no longer felt so argumentative.

It was at this time that I brought up the concept of progression into future lives. He expressed great interest in going into the future; an appointment for his progression was made. Larry was one of my first progression patients. The challenge of this new technique, combined with Larry's skeptical stance, greatly appealed to me.

On a very warm June afternoon, we began Larry's progression. At first he regressed into a past life. It was a different life than we had explored in previous sessions. I gave him the appropriate suggestions to detach himself from this scene and to go into the future. He reported a most unusual existence.

Dr. G.:   What do you see at this time?
Larry: The decompression chamber.
Dr. G.:   What is the decompression chamber used for?
Larry: They are using it to help the divers rest.
Dr. G.:   Who are the divers?
Larry: Builders. The new city under the ocean is being built, and these divers must spend some time in the decompression chamber before they can resume normal functioning.

Dr. G.:   What is your name?
Larry: Zeku.
Dr. G.:   What year is this?
Larry: 2542.
Dr. G.:   How old are you, Zeku?
Larry: Fourteen.

Zeku was the son of a scientist who headed a team of technicians in charge of construction of an underwater city. The scientist's name was Lus-Lu, and to say he was Zeku's father requires some explaining. Genetics had made some rather significant advances in this civilization. It seems that the egg of the mother was removed by a special surgical techinque and placed in a test tube of some kind. The sperm of the proposed father was then analyzed for genetic content and compared to that of the egg. Any undesirable genetic qualities were then altered or removed from the sperm or the ovum by the use of very fine lasers and some form of radiation treatment.

After the appropriate alterations were made, the egg was then placed back in the mother's uterus and the pregnancy continued as usual. It was not illegal to have children without scientific intervention, but most people chose this method to avoid having intellectually or physically inferior offspring.

The scene quickly changed and Zeku next found himself in a desert environment. It was very difficult to obtain information until after the patient regained his orientation to the scene.

Dr. G.:   Why are you in the desert?
Larry: It's so hot. I don't like it. My father wants me to become a scientist but I don't want to do this type of work. I'm here with the Weather Control Team to rebuild the thermal transformer.
Dr. G.:   What does a thermal transformer do?
Larry: It regulates the weather. The humidity as well as the ground temperature are controlled by the transformer. It malfunctioned and my team was sent to repair it.

It seemed that Zeku was twenty years old now and he was training to be part of a Weather Control Team. This civilization had discovered a way to control the weather by setting up a series of thermal transformers all around the world. The average temperature was set between 70° and 75° Fahrenheit all year round. Zeku was not doing very well in his studies and wanted to leave the Weather Control Team. Lus-Lu wouldn't permit him to quit, so Zeku unhappily went on this assignment.

I couldn't get much information about the form of government that existed at this time. It appears there were no separate nations, just one society. The entire population of the world was less than one billion people due to two major events. One was a major geographical alteration of the earth's surface by earthquakes, tidal waves and other natural disasters. Much land was submerged and many of our present-day nations were completely destroyed. A second factor was a small scale nuclear war which occurred in the 24th century, and a much larger war in the 25th century which destroyed much of the world's population. Buildings weren't primarily affected, but human life was terminated in great numbers. Peace was finally achieved and now the world functioned harmoniously for technological advancement and education.

Zeku didn't seem to care much about anything. Unlike Larry, he had no great interest in current events but just wanted to be left alone. I next progressed Zeku to the age of 24.

Dr. G.:   Zeku, do you have a girlfriend?
Larry: Yes. I see a great deal of Kara.
Dr. G.:   What kind of work does Kara do?
Larry: She works for the Nuclear Sanitation Team. Her job is to monitor the water supply and to test certain foods for radiation poisoning.

As a result of the 25th century nuclear war, much radiation contamination still remained and presented certain dangers to the public. The government, known as The League of One, consisted of various specialty teams, each with specific functions to perform. Zeku's team required extensive traveling, separating him too often from Kara, so he decided to quit his job and was reassigned to a form of maintenance supervisor at a space port. These space ports represented transportation centers much like our airports and train stations. The difference here was the type of transportation that existed. You could be beamed from one place to another, which consisted of disassembling the molecules of your body and reassembling them at the other transportation center at your destination. (I was to hear of this again later, during Harry Martin's progression into the future.) Another mode of transportation was some sort of nuclear-powered mini jet aircraft. These small crafts transported 25 to 50 people to various small cities. The third form of transportation was a very large nuclear powered aircraft that carried between 150 and 500 people to major cities only.

Dr. G.:   Zeku, what does your job consist of?
Larry: I monitor the operation of Transportation Depot R-16.
Dr. G.:   Who takes care of the daily maintenance tasks?
Larry: D-7164 and E-431.
Dr. G.:   What are D-7164 and E-431?
Larry: They are androids constructed and programmed for performing all of the specific cleaning and organizational tasks.
Dr. G.:   Are there any other uses for androids?
Larry: Yes. Androids perform all of the menial tasks. The League assigns millions of these androids all over the world to perform all types of lifting, cleaning, general maintenance and very specific functions. They accompany all of the teams on every kind of assignment.
Dr. G.:   Do you like your present assignment?
Larry: It's all right. I can spend more time with Kara and I don't have to be in a laboratory day after day.

Zeku's mother died and he and his father saw very little of each other. Zeku described many technological advancements of his civilization. It seemed that mental telepathy was being developed as a form of communication. A pill of some kind was created to place a person in a psychic state (probably some form of chemically induced hypnosis) that allowed for a free exchange of thoughts. This was an experimental technique, but according to Zeku, much progress was being made.

Farming had undergone tremendous change. Very large forms of vegetation were developed by geneticists, resulting in fruits the size of cars. Lasers were used to divide and process the foodstuff. Education was a part of everyday life. The average worker spent only three six-hour days working. The rest of the time was for leisure. Many vacations were taken each year and life seemed to be rather easy. The average life span was over 125 years.

As a result of the nuclear war of the 25th century, mutants existed. These mutants were treated with very fine laser beams, though these treatments weren't always successful.

An information pill which contained all the new scientific achievements, new items of general interest, and all of the latest advancements was available daily. A type of indestructible plastic was used extensively in construction of vehicles, buildings and machinery.

Much research was being done on interplanetary and inter-galactic travel. This society had made contact with other planets, but the time it took to reach these planets was still enormous. The molecular beaming procedure that I referred to earlier was only used for relatively short distances. Even with nuclear powered engines and traveling at the speed of light, it still took many years to reach other galaxies.

I next progressed Zeku to a very significant event in his life. He was now 27 years old.

Dr. G.: Where are you now?

Larry: I am working at R-16 but I am worried.

Dr. G.: What are you worried about?

Larry: There have been problems with some of the molecular transport units.

Dr. G.: What specifically is the problem?

Larry: There have been additional time lapses between transport sites. It is unsafe to be disassembled for longer than five minutes.

Dr. G.: Who is responsible for their proper functioning?

Larry: I am. If I can't repair them soon, some people are going to get hurt.

Dr. G.: Why don't you just shut them down for repair?

Larry: I can't do that without the proper authority. Since these units work properly most of the time and since this malfunction is not consistent or predictable, I could get into trouble for shutting them down.

Dr. G.: Why is that?

Larry: These units are used by many people every day and I
              must keep them operational.
Dr. G.:   Is that the only reason you're worried?
Larry: No. My supervisor Deui will probably transfer me if I
              can't solve this problem. He has already transferred
              Treva and Graf and I know that I'm next to go. If he
              transfers me, I won't be able to see Kara often.
Dr. G.:   So, what are you going to do?
Larry: I'm going to stay here tonight and work on all of these
              units until they work perfectly.
Dr. G.:   Are you going to do this alone?
Larry: Yes. The android units are shut off after the normal
              workday ends.

Zeku described a scene in which he was busy at work on the
molecular transport units. It was very difficult for him to work
without the aid of the androids, and he seemed very stressed
and tense.

Dr. G.:   What is happening now, Zeku?
Larry: I think I solved the malfunction problem. There seems
              to be a defective circuit by the main power unit, and
              I'm going to repair it quickly and test all of the units.
Dr. G.:   Did you repair the defective circuit?
Larry: I'm working on the circuit now. I'm very tired but I
              know I'm right. I've attached the new circuit and. . . .

There was silence for the next minute or so. I found out what
had happened shortly. It seemed that in the process of replacing
the defective circuit, Zeku had accidentally activated the transport unit. His molecules were disassembled and never reassembled.
He died a painless death. He reported the usual sensations of
floating and freedom from all discomforts that patients describe
in regression following their death.

I brought Larry back to the present and discussed the event
with him. It was a rather long session and I felt somewhat drained
after it was over. Larry felt drained himself, but he was im-
mensely happy with the experience. I don't know whether he
fully accepted the idea of progression, but he now thought it
worthy of consideration.

In his past lives, Larry was argumentative and stubborn. This resulted in a violent death during the 16th century in England. Presently, this tendency toward disagreement caused him marital problems and personality conflicts with his employees. Overcoming this negative trait improved Larry's personal and professional lives.

Larry has always been interested in current events and logical scientific thought processes. He expressed his interest in progression even though he was initially skeptical about hypnosis. As Zeku, he didn't care for science or much or anything else, except Kara. Zeku showed a lack of responsibility but when it came to the molecular transport unit's repair he accepted this challenge well. The pressure he was under was similar to Larry's environment in his 20th century position as a manager of large numbers of employees. Even though it resulted in his death Zeku accepted a great responsibility. Larry also accepted a great responsibility when he gave up his argumentative trait. The karmic lesson was learned and probably won't have to be dealt with again.

CHAPTER EIGHTEEN

WHAT IS IT LIKE TO DIE?

Death is a depressing, fearful topic to most people. Yet, we all know that death, like taxes, is unavoidable. In this chapter I will explore accounts of death from my patients who have been regressed or progressed. In nearly every past-life regression I have participated in and in many I present in this book there is an inevitable moment of death to explore—and in each patient's account, the findings are always much the same.

Actually, death itself is not a traumatic experience. It is the birth process that is traumatic. Imagine for a moment that you are very ill and lying in a hospital bed. Then imagine your astral body lifting out and all of a sudden you are dead. It takes hours, days, or even weeks to realize that you are, in fact, dead. That is hardly traumatic. All pain and other discomforts are completely removed at the moment of death.

Now imagine yourself being born. The newborn has just acquired a subconscious and has left its cozy womb for a bright, sterile environment that is totally different and most uncomfortable compared to what it has been used to for nine months. The newborn is slapped, footprinted, suctioned, swabbed, processed, and totally dependent on strangers in white uniforms for its very survival. There is no direct data on the actual pain of the birth process, but imagine ice cold steel forceps around your head, or a premature delivery. Personally, birth seems more intimidating to me than dying.

Eliminating the fear of death is one of the greatest benefits of regression and progression therapy. The realization that death is not an end but a birth into a larger, fuller and more meaningful life is quite beautiful. Death is merely an exchange of an old body for a new one. Death signifies the beginning of a rest and reevaluation period. It is a form of recreation and renewal. It is a transition state, not a state of termination. Death may be hard to explain or to understand, but it is not to be feared.

Many problems patients ask me to help them with have their origins in past-life death scenes. Once these death scenes are re-lived, the symptoms disappear accordingly. A traumatic death, such as falling off a cliff, could result in a fear of heights. Reliving this fall often results in the elimination of the phobia.

For the time being I would like you to put aside thoughts of Heaven, Hell, and even Purgatory. Put aside religious convictions and open your mind to what I have to say. Of course, you don't have to accept this information. All I ask is that you consider it with an open mind.

When we die we are really not dead in the common use of the word. We may be non-functional on the earth plane but we are quite functional on other planes. We exist then on the astral plane, and eventually we will enter the white light and end up on the soul plane. So, what we think of as death is really shifting to another plane of existence.

Before I go into details about the parapsychological explanations of death, let me give you some medical facts. The cells in our body are dying and being replaced constantly. One of the purposes of the sleep state, at least from a medical point of view, is to re-create the many millions of cells that are killed during each day that we live. We are also replacing lost energy during sleep. Scientists tell us that about every nine months, each and every one of our cells has been replaced at least once.

So, technically, we die every nine months. Our body is completely different than it was one year ago and will be completely different at this time next year. We obviously don't feel dead and are able to function quite nicely. The process of cell replacement continues along so smoothly that we are not aware of anything different happening. It is our physical perception that is being fooled into thinking that the body is unchanged from year to year.

THE EXPERIENCE OF DEATH

What seems to happen at death is that you experience, at least initially, what you *expect* to experience. In other words, your expectations of what death should be like seem to affect the actual experience or perception of death. A belief in the fires of Hell or the clouds of Heaven will often manifest themselves, temporarily at least. Fortunately these fantasies disappear quickly and you are joined by Masters and Guides. These angel-like entities will try and help you adjust to the astral plane. They will guide you into a gradual realization that you have died and it is time to move on. You may not even accept the fact that you have died at first, because you really won't feel much different. There is, however, one very significant difference: you are now totally free of any discomfort. Your new environment will be far less limiting than that of the physical plane, which you have just left.

On the astral plane, you may find yourself in the presence of dead relatives or friends. Telepathy is the rule now, so that your true feelings toward that friend or relative will be made known, and vice versa. There is no hypocrisy on the astral plane.

When you go to sleep every night, out-of-body experiences occur and simulate the death experience. This simulated death state is merely training for later. Dreams of flying or falling are conscious remnants of this astral projection.

I alluded earlier to the white light. This white light is an express train to the soul plane—the plane where you will evaluate your past life and choose your next one. Your Masters and Guides and "dead" relatives and friends will advise you to enter this white light. If you do, then all is well and good. But, as I've mentioned before, if you don't, you become what is known as a "troubled spirit" and remain on the astral plane, unsure of who you are and what you are supposed to be doing. You can be observed on the earth plane as a ghost or you can be unobserved and just wander around aimlessly. You will be reminded again and again by your Masters and Guides to enter the white light. But nothing can force you to do so.

Think of it this way. You have just died. Perhaps the moments preceding death were a very traumatic experience. You are immersed with expectations of Heaven or Hell. Now some unknown entity tries to convince you to enter this blinding white light. You are frightened and resist. Remember that the soul always has free will. It's not difficult to see how someone might be hesitant to jump out of the frying pan and into the proverbial fire, but the white light absolutely must be entered in order to reach the soul plane. The task is now before you. What is real? What is imaginary? What is good? What is evil? Who are the good guys? Who or what are the bad guys? These questions may have to be answered before the soul will decide to enter the white light.

The soul will use its judgment as to who or what to trust. It is the soul alone that will make this decision. The state of mind at death, the karmic cycle, the environment on the astral plane and other factors will help to make this determination. It may take a few hours or a century for this answer. A more experienced soul that just completed a positive life, karmically, would require less time and would much more likely make the correct decision.

Interestingly, there is rarely any form of correlation between a patient's religion and his or her experience of death. In other words, it doesn't seem to matter whether the patient is an agnostic, atheist, Christian, Jew, Hindu, or any other belief; the experiences reported to me are similar.

There are many types of reactions that my patients report to me when they relive a death scene in a past life regression. I will discuss only the most common descriptions my patients have given of the death experience.

CROSSING OVER

First, a floating sensation is almost always described. Whatever physical discomforts the patient may have felt at the moment of death are completely gone. There is no pain or any other feeling at the moment. The patient is simply floating. Feelings of inner peace and quiet, with a complete absence of fear, are quite common. The body below is now viewed as if it were no longer a part of the patient. Indeed, this is exactly the case. Let me repeat, there is absolutely no danger of the patient's really dying, even in very deep trance levels, while reliving the death experience from a past life.

Patients soon realize that they have a body, but a very different type of body, subject to very different physical laws. This astral body possesses the ability to do many things that the physical body cannot. For example, this astral body can move through walls and doors and travel thousands of miles in a matter of seconds. Time is not registered at this level, and the astral body possesses complete knowledge of the former life and can even read the minds of other people who were involved in that life.

THE SILVER CORD

One constant observation that people have reported to me is the presence of a "silver cord." Theoretically, when one experiences an astral projection not related to a death experience, there is a silver cord that attaches to the back of the head of the astral body and to the solar plexus region of the physical body here on earth. As long as this silver cord is unbroken, the patient's physical body is still alive. Upon death this silver cord is broken.

DEATH SOUNDS

Another observation is auditory. People hear all sorts of noises following death. Buzzing sounds that appear to originate from inside the head are commonly reported; loud ringing sounds, clicks, roars, banging noises, whistling and musical sounds. One theory that has been proposed states that each plane has a characteristic combination of light and sound, and this will change as one ascends or descends to different planes. The individual's vibrational rate is also changing. At this time many bright colors are often seen. They change frequently and seem to move by at a very rapid rate.

THE TUNNEL

The feeling of moving through a long, dark tunnel is, in my opinion, the most fascinating and important observation of the death experience. Some patients use the term "vacuum." It seems as if the patient is being drawn into this tunnel, and once in this dark structure they are transported to the other side, or astral plane. This may be comparable to a time warp or a black hole.

When I regress or progress patients, I usually suggest they imagine themselves entering a tunnel which has a bright white light at the end. I suggest that there is a fork at the end of the tunnel. If the patient takes the right fork he ends up in a past life. A future life would be the destination if the left fork were taken. This technique is very successful and one of the most commonly used methods of guiding a patient into a past or future life. Whether in a hypnotic state or death, the tunnel clearly seems to represent the passageway to the next level.

THE PRESENCE OF OTHERS

Once the patient is able to stabilize him- or herself after emerging from the tunnel and adjust to the floating sensation, the presence of others is noted. By "others," I am referring to Masters and Guides who come to offer their help and guidance. Also, the patient may report seeing "dead" relatives and friends who try to help. All communication is by telepathy at this time. A feeling of warmth, security and inner peace is usually prevalent. The patient is made to feel loved; all fears of death are removed.

THE WHITE LIGHT

The white light is the culmination of the death experience. The patient is shown the white light, which at this time will appear as an almost blinding, yet peaceful aura of pure white light. This light is very similar to the image used in various healing techniques on the earth plane. By imagining that you are surrounding the damaged part of the body with this white light, patients have facilitated their own healing. On the astral plane, the patient will benefit most if he or she enters the white light, where they will be taken to the soul plane to re-evaluate this last life and choose the next one. But, as I have mentioned before, not everyone chooses to enter the white light immediately and may wander around the lower astral plane for many earth years or even centuries before they finally do enter.

INDIVIDUAL VARIATIONS

The experiences of death don't always follow the order I've described. Also, there may be time lags between each step. Some people accept the death state quickly and easily. Others require more time and guidance before they will even accept the idea of death, let alone enter the white light.

Remember, it is your expectations of what the death state is supposed to be that will affect the actual experience. If you expect to be surrounded by haloed angels in white robes playing harps, your Masters and Guides will do their very best to create that scene for you because they know that it will make you feel comfortable. It is only when you are comfortable that these higher entities will inform you about where you are and who they are and what you are supposed to be doing.

The main point of this chapter is to demonstrate that death is not an experience to fear. Perhaps it is not something to look forward to, but it is not to be feared.

Accounts of death from past-life regressions may not be sufficient evidence for some of you. There have been numerous reports of patients pronounced clinically dead who eventually survived. When asked of their experiences, they have reported startlingly similar observations to those presented here. Yet, these people experiencing near-death have usually never heard of past-life regression.

If people from different religious backgrounds who are regressed, and people who have clinically died and returned to life, all report similar experiences, the correspondences between these descriptions are more than coincidental. Yet, in the final analysis, you must form your own opinions. Death is an experience you will face many times. It is up to you to interpret this concept to fit your own particular beliefs.

My intention is to remove much of the misconception about the experience, so that when the time comes for you to die, your experience will be as peaceful and serene as possible. In previous chapters, you have seen many reassuringly similar accounts of the death experience. If, by reading this chapter, you have shed even one aspect of your fear, my efforts have been worth while.

CHAPTER NINETEEN

KARMA: WHEN DOES IT ALL END?

Does the cycle of birth and rebirth ever end? Of course it does. One of the purposes of this book is to show you how to improve your own karmic cycle. By showing you that you will live again, and that your future life will be far more pleasant and fulfilling if you follow the laws of karma wisely, I hope to help you help yourself.

Some of you may still have strong feelings of disbelief, skepticism, and mistrust. Others may gain additional support for their beliefs and hope for the future from reading this book. My hope is that you keep your mind open. It is not hypnotherapists who heal, it is you who have the ultimate responsibility. Past life regression and progression into future lives allow you to expand and explore your awareness and eliminate fear, anxiety, depression and other negative tendencies, as well as the fear of death.

Hypnotherapy is neither magic nor a panacea. It is a way to help shape the future. By creating your own reality with the knowledge from your subconscious and superconscious minds, you can positively affect your present and future lives.

Karma is simply cause and effect. It is totally just. One might describe it as a practical code of ethics. You are in control of your karma. Every soul plays the part of judge and jury. You can only fool yourself—temporarily. Karma teaches you that you have only yourself to blame or credit for your life. Do not look to somebody else as a scapegoat. To thine own self be true.

There must be a system to explain our happiness and distress. Some mechanism must be at work to determine who gets what and why. Karma, with its mechanism of reincarnation, is the best answer I have found. Luck doesn't explain the content or the quality of our lives; coincidence doesn't explain them. Karma does. Do unto others is a reality and a positive way to live.

With technological advancement there is a trend toward depersonalization in our world. Our lives seem to be numbered, sorted, stamped, and processed without a human mind to mediate the action. But self-identification is still within us all. By tapping our subconscious we can find out who we really are and what makes us tick. It is when we reach our threshold of tolerance of the processed world around us that we rebel with violence, hatred, and fear. By looking within ourselves, we can improve our individual lives and the quality of society as a whole. As a result, we can have an optimistic vision of our collective future.

We sometimes forget that there is a God. God doesn't punish us. We punish ourselves. As a man sows, so shall he reap. We will find ourselves in far more pleasant surroundings in our next life if we make the most of our opportunities to serve our fellow men and women now. If we steal in this life, our possessions will be stolen from us. If we kill, we too shall die by violence. We will escape our karmic cycle when we end it by learning, loving, and doing.

We have a choice. The soul always has free will. We can choose to do good or evil, right or wrong. We choose our future lives. Who would choose to kill, rape, steal, or cheat if he or she realized the karmic implications? Learning to use these principles of karma to better ourselves, we are bettering the future for us all.

Many people ask me to help them speed up their karmic cycles so that they won't have to come back again. I can't do that. Only you can do that. After reading this book, you have the basic knowledge to speed up your karmic cycle or do anything that you set your subconscious mind to do. Be honest, truthful, and faithful to your own code of ethics. If you follow this simple advice, you are well on your way to the higher planes.

This entire process will end when you fulfill your karma. When you learn all the lessons you have to learn and show kindness and unselfish love to all those with whom you come into contact, the cycle will end. When it ends, you will go beyond the soul plane to the higher planes and, eventually, to God. Karma is merely a process of evolution, of achieving greater levels of perfection. It gives life.

I like to think of karma as opportunities. As one faces each new opportunity, new choices and decisions must be made. It requires much courage to face our shortcomings and an equal amount of wisdom to do something constructive about them. We have these choices. We can dictate our future by acting appropriately in the present. Completing our karmic cycle is not easy, but it is within our grasp. By reviewing each opportunity objectively and by being aware of our karma—with the knowledge gained from past and future lives—imagine how much improved our present lives could be.

Learn these lessons well, and you will have taken the next step toward your destiny.

CHAPTER TWENTY

QUESTIONS AND ANSWERS ABOUT PAST AND FUTURE LIVES HYPNOTHERAPY

Q. Why can't people consciously recall past lives?
A. All memories about our past and future lives are stored in the subconscious mind. This subconscious mind functions independently of the conscious mind. Since your conscious mind died along with the body when your last life ended, you start each new life with a virgin conscious mind. This conscious mind cannot recall any of its past lives simply because it has no memories of them.

It is only your subconscious or superconscious mind that can remember your past or future lives. This mechanism is actually quite protective. Because the mind is exposed to more than one million pieces of new information every day of our lives, think of what it would be like to consciously recall all of this information from our present as well as our past and future lives at any one moment.

There are certain clues to our past lives that we do experience consciously. We all have certain natural talents, likes and dislikes. Certain intuitive tendencies are remnants from past lives. When we dream we often see scenes from past lives. Spontaneous regressions occur to many people in their dreams. Even though we do not consciously remember our past or future lives, there are experiences that give us the knowledge that we have lived before and will live again.

Q. Has anyone not had a past life?
A. There are very few people who request regressions or progressions from me that are not able to achieve one or the other. This does not mean that they have had no past lives. It simply

means that I am unable to use hypnosis on them successfully to obtain this information.

When I speak directly to a patient's subconscious or super-conscious in trance, I usually receive past or future life data. Never has a patient's superconscious mind denied the existence of past lives. I do not believe, nor have I obtained any evidence that anyone living today is here for the first time.

Q. Have people been animals in past lives?
A. In all of the regressions and progressions I have performed, I have never had a patient relate a life to me in any other than a human form. The only exceptions to this are regressions of "light people," as described in Chapter 7. Even these "light people" represent human forms, rather than plants or animals.

In certain Hindu and Buddhist schools of Eastern philosophy, transmigration is mentioned. According to these Eastern beliefs, our soul first incarnates as minerals, then plants, then lower animals, and finally the human form is inhabited. This trans-migration from minerals to human form is not accepted even by most of the Eastern philosophers today. I personally don't accept it and I have never obtained any evidence to support this theory.

The extraterrestrial concept of reincarnation has gained much acceptance today in many parapsychological circles. This concept is described in Chapter 3 and it nullifies the transmigration theory.

Q. What methods other than hypnosis can help reveal past and future lives?
A. Karmic astrological charts can be constructed for you with the time, place and date of your birth. This chart will tell you much about your past, present and future lives. It will give you great insight into your sub-cycle as well as your total karmic cycle.

Psychics and mediums can often read your Akashic records or at least communicate with your Masters and Guides. In any event, much information concerning your past, present and future lives can be obtained in this way, too.

Another way we obtain karmic information is from spon-taneous regressions and progressions. This experience is infre-quent and totally unpredictable, but it is an avenue for karmic data. Dreams represent still another avenue. During the dream state you can witness scenes from past and future lives and consciously remember them upon awakening.

Group meditation is advocated by some. I am not convinced that there is much difference between meditation and hypnosis, except that meditation works better with groups of people and is far less efficient than hypnosis. Both techniques are examples of alpha brain waves.

Automatic writing represents still another method. In this technique you sit quietly with a pencil or pen in your hand resting on some paper. Your hand will move and your subconscious mind will communicate with you by directing your hand movements in the form of words and phrases. I have used this technique with certain patients for various forms of therapy, but I personally have not used it to retrieve information about past or future lives.

Another method is conscious contact with your Masters and Guides. This is quite rare, but there are entirely sane people who claim this ability, and report that they have received information about their past or future lives in this way. Seances represent still another way to obtain this information. I have no personal experience with these phenomena. Apparently, entities from past, present, or future lives can be communicated with directly by way of a seance.

Q. Why are children more likely to remember past lives without the aid of hypnosis?
A. Children don't have as many hang-ups as adults. They are not bothered by what people think. Most importantly, the nervous system is not fully formed in a child until the age of about six. There are small openings in the skull that theoretically allow the soul or subconscious mind to escape and communicate directly with the child. Children, then, are able to consciously remember past lives without having to be formally hypnotized. These openings close by the age of 2½. There have also been many cases of children having spontaneous past life regressions and other psychic experiences. Children see ghosts and have many more astral projections during daytime hours than adults. Their parents tend to discourage these episodes, which is unfor-

tunate. Children actually make excellent hypnotic patients, and some very interesting regressions and progressions result from working with them. One of the many exciting things about working with children is that the information obtained often shows knowledge and the vocabulary of an adult. There seems to me to be no other explanation of how these children acquired such knowledge than through past lives.

Q. How can the present population be explained by reincarnation?
A. One theory states that a soul is able to occupy more than one body at a time. If one soul occupied three bodies in the year 3000 B.C., for example, and if each of these sub-souls occupied three additional bodies each, it would not be difficult to see how one soul could occupy one and a half million bodies in the matter of thirteen lifetimes.

Q. When does the soul enter the body of a newborn?
A. Although the soul can come and go as it pleases during the entire course of the pregnancy, it is usually within 24 hours before or after birth that the soul makes its grand entrance. Remember that the soul leaves our body every night during our sleep state. The soul is never permanently trapped within the body.

Q. Does the bible mention reincarnation?
A. Yes, it most certainly does. In the third century A.D. there was a teacher by the name of Origen. He promoted the concept of reincarnation. In 533 A.D., however, a church council met in Constantinople. At this meeting, which was not even attended by the Pope of Rome, Origen's teachings were condemned and most of the references to reincarnation were removed from the Bible. Fortunately, some are still present in the Old and New Testaments including:

 1. John 9:1-3
 "And as Jesus passed by, he saw a man which was blind from birth. And his Disciples asked him saying, "Master, who did sin, this man or his parents, that he was born blind?" Jesus answered, "Neither has this man sinned nor his

parents. He was born blind that the works of God should be manifest in him.''

2. Obadiah 1:15
''As thou has done, it shall be done unto thee; thy reward shall return thine own head.''

3. Revelation 3:12
''Him that overcometh will I make a pillar in the temple of my God and he shall go no more out.''

4. Wisdom of Solomon 8:19–20
''Now I was a good child by nature, and a good soul fell to my lot. Nay, rather being good, I came into a body undefiled.''

5. Isaiah 26:19
''Thy dead men shall live, together with my dead body shall they arise. Awake and sing, ye that dwell in dust for . . . the earth shall cast out the dead.''

6. Daniel 12:2
''And many of them that sleep in the dust of the earth shall awake, some to everlasting life, and some to shame and everlasting contempt.''

7. Matthew 17:1–13
''And after six days Jesus took with him Peter and James and John his brother, and led them up a high mountain apart. And he was transfigured before them, and his face shown like the sun, and his garments became white as light. And behold, there appeared to them Moses and Eli'jah talking with him. And Peter said to Jesus, 'Lord, it is well that we are here; if you wish, I will make three booths here, one for you and one for Moses and one for Eli'jah.' He was still speaking, when lo, a bright cloud overshadowed them, and a voice from the cloud said, ''This is my beloved Son, with whom I am well pleased; listen to him.'' When the disciples heard this, they fell on their faces, and were filled with awe. But Jesus came and touched them, saying 'Rise, and have no fear.' And when they lifted up their eyes, they saw no one but Jesus only. And as they were coming down the mountain, Jesus commanded them, 'Tell no one the vision, until the Son of man is raised from the dead.' And the

disciples asked him, 'Then why do the scribes say that first Eli'jah must come?' He replied, 'Eli'jah does come, and he is to restore all things; but I tell you that Eli'jah has already come, and they did not know him, but did to him whatever they pleased. So also the Son of man will suffer at their hands.' Then the disciples understood that he was speaking to them of John the Baptist.

8. Job 33:15–18

"In a dream, in a vision of the night, when deep sleep falleth upon men, in slumberings upon the bed; then he openeth the ears of men, and sealeth their instruction, that he may withdraw man from his purpose, and hide pride from man. He keepeth back his soul from the pit, and his life from perishing by the sword."

9. Other reincarnation references:

    a. "Whatsoever a man soweth, that shall he also reap." St. Paul (Gal. 6:7)

    b. St. Augustine in Confessions 1:6

    c. St. Jerome in his Letter to Avitus

There are cases today of people in the Roman Catholic Church accepting reincarnation without being declared heretical. (An example of this is the late Cardinal Mercier [Prelate of Belgian Catholics] and the late Dean Inge of St. Paul's Cathedral in London.

Q. Does a belief in reincarnation conflict with a belief in God?
A. I hope that throughout this book you have noted my many references to God. My work as a hypnotherapist specializing in past life regression and progression into future lives has only strengthened my personal belief in God. It is hard for me to imagine someone working in this field not having a very strong belief in God. If more and more people studied parapsychology, especially the karmic cycle, I'm confident that we would see a renaissance in monotheism (a belief in one God).

Q. Does one always improve in his next life?
A. Not necessarily. If you fail to learn the lessons that you are supposed to master, then you will have to face these same lessons in either this or a future life. Also, in the process of dealing with

other entities, you could incur negative karma. This would add
to your karmic cycle rather than help it. Since the soul always
has free will, you are not guaranteed improvement with each life.
The fact that we have thousands of lives and still much karma to
work out highly suggests that we do not constantly improve in
our karmic cycles.

Q. Why are progressions more difficult than regressions?
A. I am not sure why progressions are more difficult. Perhaps
it is because we are all programmed to believe that the future
hasn't occurred yet. Another reason might be that the actual
mechanism involved disorients our subconscious mind's thought
process. I hope further research will give us some insight to this
question.

Q. Do we ever change sex in our karmic cycle?
A. We must change sex at least once in order to complete our
karmic cycle. Even though we do change sex at least once, most
of our lives are lived as one sex. This change of sex roles in our
karmic cycles offers one possible explanation for homosexuality.
Another possible karmic explanation for homosexuality is that
people have been ridiculed, ostracized and punished for sexual
behavior in previous lives.

**Q. How do you know these past lives are not figments of the
imagination? Might not some of your patients just be making
these lives up?**
A. My patients are able to overcome negative habits and eliminate phobias as a result of past-lives regressions. If they were
simply imagining these scenes, these problems would not disappear. The remission of symptoms seems proof enough to me.
Second, the lives my patients report to me are hardly compli-
mentary to themselves. Most of these lives are tedious and dull,
rather than glamorous, hardly the kind of lives one would fanta-
size about to enhance one's self-image.

In addition, I have never regressed a patient who lived the life
of a celebrated historical figure. This only adds to the validity of
hypnotic regression. One would naturally question the possibility
of regressing Napoleon, Cleopatra, and George Washington all

within the same year. The odds against regressing a famous person from history are astronomically high. Since I have performed thousands of regressions and none of these accounts have been of historical figures, I feel that this precludes the idea of patients using their imagination. But you must make your own determination about what you accept when it comes to karma.

Q. How do I find a qualified hypnotherapist?
A. I would like to close this book with some advice to those of you who will seek out hypnosis to explore past or future lives. Although I know of no case in which hypnosis has ever harmed anyone, I highly recommend that you seek out a qualified hypnotherapist. The term hypnotherapist is usually used by someone with a doctorate in the health sciences. It may be a D.D.S. (such as myself), it may be a Ph.D. (such as a psychologist), or an M.D. (a physician), or other health professional.

The term *hypnotist* refers to a person without professional training, including their training in hypnosis, which rarely exceeds four days. The reason I recommend a doctor is because doctors live by very strong ethical codes. A lay hypnotist may or may not have these standards. Second, our background includes much training in psychology and other behavioral sciences.

The second quality I would look for in a hypnotherapist is a very extensive background in the field of parapsychology. He or she should be knowledgeable about all aspects of karma and able to answer your questions and offer the appropriate guidance.

The third quality to look for is experience. The therapist should have done regressions or progressions many, many times before. They should also be experienced in shielding (white light protection) techniques, which should, without exception, precede any regression or progression.

Fourth, trust your instinct about the therapist. If they are qualified but you don't like or trust them, leave immediately. Not only will you not succeed with that particular therapist, but you might just be susceptible to his or her negative karma.

Since 1958, the American Medical Association has formally accepted hypnosis as a reputable clinical aid. The British Medical Association accepted hypnosis in 1955. No longer are hypnotherapists thought of as charlatans or stage entertainers. When I first began practicing hypnotherapy, patients would seek my services as a last resort, usually after traditional medicine and psychotherapy had failed. Today I'm more often approached initially, before other traditional forms of therapy are considered. Of course, I refer my patients to physicians to rule out possible physiological causes of their complaints. When the physical causes of illness are eliminated, I begin my therapy. Any therapist you meet should take this clinical approach.

ABOUT THE AUTHOR

Dr. Goldberg graduated from Southern Connecticut State College in June 1970, Magna Cum Laude, earning a B.A. degree in Biology and Chemistry. He then attended the University of Maryland School of Dentistry, receiving his Doctor of Dental Surgery degree in May 1974. Upon completion of a general practice residency program in dentistry, he set up both a general dental and hypnosis practice in Baltimore where he currently practices. In 1984, Dr. Goldberg received his M.S. in Counseling Psychology from Loyola College.

The American Society of Clinical Hypnosis trained Dr. Goldberg in the techniques and clinical applications of hypnosis in January, 1975. This organization trains only licensed Dentists, Physicians, and Psychologists in the use of hypnosis.

Dr. Goldberg has appeared on many television and radio shows throughout the country. While on the air, he has conducted many live past life regressions and has hosted a talk show on parapsychology on WBAL radio in Baltimore. Through the use of lectures, television and radio appearances, and newspaper articles (including interviews with Time and the Washington Post), he has been able to educate many people as to the benefits of hypnosis. Dr. Goldberg keeps his hypnosis practice separate from his dental practice, although he does work with patients concerning their fears of dental treatment and pain control. He has conducted thousands of these past life regressions and progressions and none of his patients have ever been harmed through this technique. In addition, Dr. Goldberg distributes cassette tapes to teach people self-hypnosis and to guide them into past and future lives.

In addition, Dr. Goldberg gives lectures and seminars on hypnosis and regression and progression therapy. Dr. Goldberg is also a consultant to local police departments and the media (local and network). Lastly, Dr. Goldberg teaches a fully accredited course in clinical hypnosis at Essex Community College in Baltimore.

For information on self-hypnosis tapes, speaking engagements, or private sessions, Dr. Goldberg can be contacted directly by writing to:

Dr. Bruce Goldberg, Inc., 4708 Beaconsfield Drive, Baltimore, MD 21236
Telephone No.: (301) 256-7022